Tradition!

To my mother, Maria Petropoulos Kockos,
my teacher in the kitchen and in life.
To her I will always be profoundly grateful.

There is no sincerer love than the love of food.

—George Bernard Shaw

Contents

Foreword

I remember the day when, as a young teenager, a few of us encouraged my mother to open a coffee shop and serve her delicious traditional Greek dishes and sweets; we were certain it would be a success. She perked at the idea, but without the resources for such an endeavor she dismissed the notion.

As time went on, I decided I would learn to cook all my mother's recipes before she could no longer do so herself. As a first-generation Greek American on my mother's side and second-generation on my father's, continuity matters. So I embraced the call to preserve the recipes from my childhood.

While observing her ways in the kitchen, I took notes the same careful way I did in high school and college. But it wasn't always easy documenting the method and the amount. Though her formula was at hand, my mother also operated intuitively. "About this much" or "until it feels this way," she would say. I had a lot to learn.

Later in years as my mother's health declined, I decided to honor her by writing a cookbook. "With my recipes?" she asked.

"Yes, Mom," I replied; she smiled. In the middle of this endeavor, my mother died after a long struggle with vascular dementia.

Soon after, a friend gave me a booklet of prayer hymns *(akathist)* for those whose loved ones have departed. A verse from one of these hymns recites, "May good deeds be multiplied in her name."[1] Although the coffee shop never came to fruition, it is my sincere hope that in sharing her many recipes contained in this cookbook, they produce goodness and joy for you and your loved ones.

Introduction

When I turned seventeen, my mother gave me a yellow accordion-style case to store my new recipes. I still use it all these years later, but like an old friend it now wears wrinkles. The flaxen grosgrain ribbon ties are now grayed and smudged, and the vanilla dividers bear the color of my afternoon tea. All over, it proudly wears badges from my cooking past—grease, specks, and stains. But therein lies my heart —a collection of traditional Greek and American recipes.

What is it about time-honored dishes that make them so beloved? Every culture has them. Is it because they're instantly recognizable, and immediately spark connections with family, friends, and place? Or, that their predictability offers warmth and comfort to our rapidly changing, technologically driven world? One thing is certain. Like a pair of black-heeled pumps or blue denim jeans, classic dishes never go out of style. As for me, nothing quite satisfies my soul as much as a delectable piece of home-made Moussaka or Fresh Peach Cobbler. In *Tradition! Recipes, Tales, and More from My Greek American Life*, I share my treasured collection with you.

Most of these recipes I learned from my mother. When I was a young girl, I observed her maneuvers in the kitchen with the same enthusiasm that I watched her apply coral-red nail polish in steady strokes, or contour lipstick in thick layers while she sat at her vanity. Fortunately, she didn't mind me around. As a matter of fact, the closeness I felt during these moments laid the foundation of a lifelong, endearing relationship, and found a haven in tasty, home-cooked food.

Other recipes arrived in my yellow case as a result of a tasty meal at an aunt's, the generosity of a friend, or inspiration from a magazine clipping. Still others were born of my disappointment with the store-bought or restaurant version. But whatever the avenue, they have one thing in common—all are mouthwateringly delicious.

Besides serving as a link to my Greek American heritage, good food has also been present amidst my most pleasurable and lasting memories—the summers I lived in Greece and became enchanted by the charming vignettes of everyday life; in my grade-school cafeteria where I fell in love with traditional American food; the stories my mother told me from her childhood; the fun years I experienced with the Gourmet Club during my single years; the time I met my husband, and more. In *Tradition!* the headnotes for many of the recipes partake of my lifelong journey with food. Of these intimate accounts, some will make you laugh, and some will make you cry. But regardless, they're here for you to enjoy.

*

Now and then someone walks into my kitchen and says, "Mmmm, that smells good." Alas, I would not know. I was born without a sense of smell. My *yiayia* (grandmother) couldn't smell either, nor can our two sons. Our daughter is my nose—she has a keen one.

"How do you cook if you can't smell?" you might ask.

My reply would be: "Well, I rely on my other senses to navigate the way. For example, the sizzle of garlic and onions in the skillet informs me when it's time to stir or add another ingredient; the touch of a cantaloupe or peach signals ripeness; and the golden brown color of baked bread or cookies discerns doneness."

"Can you taste?" you wonder.

"Yes, but I can't distinguish subtle, delicate flavors in foods. Instead I prefer those with deep flavor and robust character, as in Mediterranean cuisine," I answer. Foods like olive oil, onions, garlic, cinnamon, lemons, olives, and salty cheeses suit me just fine. In *Tradition!* these ingredients are used in myriad ways.

As a matter of fact, Greek cooking shuns finicky recipes and precise techniques in favor of simple formulas and easygoing methods. Put another way, it's like the difference between a custom-tailored suit—where each stitch and seam is meticulously crafted for a perfect fit—and a loosely fitting slipcover that's welcoming and comfortable.

This latter description also suits my other favorite cuisine—traditional American

—and I consider it a seamless counterpart to the humble, provincial style of Greek cooking. Here, you'll find approximately one-third of the ninety-five recipes devoted to this fare.

So, I invite you to join me on a journey.

Whether you love Greek food but don't have the blessing of a mother's or *yiayia's* recipes, want to experiment with a different version of your own family recipe, are itching for some new ideas, or simply enjoy reading cookbooks like novels, *Tradition!* is for you. At the very least, it promises to inspire and entertain.

While the recipes in this cookbook assume some basic knowledge of cooking, all are doable. Also, because I understand firsthand the frustration that can result from murky instructions, here in *Tradition!* I've made every effort to explain the method for each recipe clearly and concisely. This might account for some of the instructions appearing lengthy, but don't be discouraged. They simply reflect my attempt at eliminating confusion. Lastly, please note the following:

1) Serving size listed for each recipe is approximate,

2) Glass measuring cups are used for wet ingredients (called wet measure), and cups and teaspoons for dry ingredients (dry measure), and

3) Any number of factors can influence the cooking time indicated on a recipe. Therefore in most cases, I have given a second measure to test for doneness, such as "until the color is golden brown."

Each recipe in *Tradition!* has been tested and retested numerous times. As for the recipe photos, I took them all myself in my kitchen using natural light and my 2 x 3-inch Sony camera. I styled each one, too. Photos from my travels to Greece and others that appear throughout the cookbook also came from the same tiny camera.

But before you begin, I encourage you to read the next few sections. There you'll discover the *real* secrets behind every successful dish in *The Be-Attitudes of Cooking.* You'll also find *The Well-Stocked Pantry,* which details the ingredients *and* reasons for filling the larder, and *The Well-Equipped Kitchen,* which reviews everything you need to make your job in the kitchen easier.

Regarding the *Appendices* located in the back of the book, they contain the following:

• *Appendix A—Being At Ease with Phyllo:* Provides information to calm your jittery nerves about working with this fine pastry dough, and encouragement to go forward confidently.

• *Appendix B—A Walk Through the Year: Your Guide to Seasonal Produce:* Lists fresh fruits and vegetables that are available month by month to assist with your menu planning.

• *Appendix C—U.S. Cooking Measurements and Conversion Tables:* Supplies data at your fingertips without having to logon (just in case you're wondering how many teaspoons equal one tablespoon, like me—no kidding).

Now, let's proceed to the next phase of our journey.

The Be-Attitudes of Cooking

Besides the ingredients listed on a recipe, lots of other essentials get added to a pot to ensure a successful outcome. No doubt, I learned these from watching my mother in her kitchen over the years. Today, they're so automatic that I'm hardly aware of them, but writing this book caused me to pause and take notice.

I'm referring to a certain mental posture, or group of attitudes, that govern the way you function in the kitchen. When implemented, they can transform a recipe into a "dish," create a boon to flavor, and enhance your experience at the same time. These attitudes invite you to *Be-Organized, Be-Engaged, Be-Bold and Corageous, Be-In Charge,* and *Be-Joyful.* Let's take a look at each one.

1. Be-Organized

Getting organized before making a recipe is like taking certain measures before setting sail. You would want to inspect the critical machinery, such as the engine and rudder, to make sure they're working properly. You would confirm the gear is safely stowed away to prevent dislodging, and also purchase what's necessary in the way of food and beverages. Taking these steps optimizes your chance for smooth sailing. So it is with cooking. Once you've found a recipe you're excited about trying, it's essential to get organized.

How? First, *become thoroughly familiar with a recipe by reading it entirely—not once but twice.* Getting comfortable with a recipe before starting eliminates any potential for surprise— or worse, panic. Then review the ingredient list. Check your pantry to see what you already have on hand, and make a list of what needs to be purchased. Next, review the method and determine if any advance preparation is required, like soaking beans overnight. Also, check to see if extra time is required during the cooking process, like refrigeration. A rough calculation of the time involved helps you budget yours accordingly.

Second, *review the tools and equipment the recipe calls for.* There are some inexpensive tools that are essential for certain tasks. Do you have them on hand? For example, if the recipe calls for a pastry brush to coat the phyllo and you don't have one, you'll need to purchase one. Regarding cooking equipment, if the recipe asks to mix the batter but your portable electric mixer is on its last legs, it's probably time for a new one. And while on the subject of mixers, if you don't already own the freestanding electric kind, maybe now's the time to consider investing in one (more on that later in this section under *The Well-Equipped Kitchen*).

Third, *Be-Organized with your time and energy.* Cooking is fun and its rewards are abundant, but let's face it, no one wants to be a kitchen martyr. Feeling overwhelmed, tired, and frustrated takes the joy away from cooking. Get into the habit of asking yourself this vital question: "What can I do ahead of time to make the job easier on myself?" For example, can you clean and chop the vegetables in the morning, cover with plastic and refrigerate until you're ready to cook them later in the afternoon? Can you prepare the meat earlier in the day? Just imagine what a lovely gift you've given yourself knowing these tasks are done and waiting for you. In short, taking action beforehand will ease your job, lower your stress level, and make you a happier cook.

This is especially true with recipes of lengthier instruction. In these instances, look for ways you can split the job into phases. For example, for the three layers in *Moussaka*, you can roast and arrange the eggplant and zucchini (phase 1) the night before and refrigerate until the next morning. Or, you can do this *and* prepare the meat filling (phases 1 and 2) and wake up to just the final phase, the béchamel sauce. What a dreamy night's sleep you'll have knowing most of the labor is behind you. In the case of *Baklava*, you can easily toast and chop the walnuts a day or two in advance, cover with plastic and refrigerate. The bottom line is, wherever possible look for ways to make the job easier—plan ahead.

Finally, *Be-Organized with your workspace.* Before beginning a recipe, optimize your chance for success by eliminating tension in your work environment. Is your sink piled high with dirty dishes? You'll have even more when you're through, so tidy up. Is your kitchen counter smothered with bills, the children's school bulletins, catalogues, old mail, and architectural plans for your upcoming remodel? If so, clear the clutter. Are you having trouble locating the baking powder in your pantry? Maybe it's time to create a better system. Is the ground cinnamon in your recipe drawer from Thanksgiving five years ago? Clean out and start fresh. When you're finished organizing your workspace you'll be calm and relaxed. Then, light a candle, turn on some pleasing music, and get started.

2. Be-Engaged

Making tasty food is not about you. Neither is it about a recipe.

Making tasty food is about the interaction between you and a recipe, and acknowledging that small acts of kindness along the way affect the outcome. This requires being engaged.

To elaborate, while possessing culinary knowledge and skill are fine qualities themselves, cooking delicious food depends on another feature even more important—your heart. And, since the essence of your heart is love, love is that special ingredient that can transform a dish from just okay to great. Why? Because love infuses your cooking with special acts of care and nurture that get added to the pot. If love isn't present, taste gets shortchanged. And let's face it, no matter how lovely a dish may look, how it tastes matters most.

So, how do you go about elevating the flavor of a dish with both craft and heart? Through *shopping*, *layering*, and *tasting*.

Shopping

First, developing flavor begins at your local market, so I urge you to buy the best quality ingredients you can afford, and, whenever possible, select fresh, seasonal fruits and vegetables (see Appendix B on page 327 for a complete listing). With the birth of California Cuisine over forty years ago, plenty has already been written on this subject, but I want to emphasize what may seem self-evident: What goes into a recipe determines what comes out, so use discernment with your purchases.

Layering

Layering is a method of overlaying one tier on top of another. Why is this important in cooking? Because doing so expands and deepens taste, and thus makes for a more interesting eating experience. Of course, not all foods need to be layered to taste good. For example, a fresh, juicy peach, an ear of sweet corn, or a ripe tomato capture marvelous flavor alone. But when it comes to developing flavor when various ingredients are used together, the art of layering is essential. The secret lies in the *manner* in which you do it.

Here's a little story about the value of layering, and how it makes a difference.

One day your friend Buffy invites you over for coffee. When you walk into her living room for the first time, you see a plain beige sofa, a large, empty coffee table, a chair nearby, and a big TV. Her beige walls are absent of decoration, and underfoot is a beige wall-to-wall carpet. You and Buffy enjoy some pleasant conversation in the living room over a cup of coffee, and soon it's time to leave. Though Buffy was a gracious hostess, you're not sure whether you want to return—the ambiance felt bland and sterile. Next time you'll suggest meeting at the local café instead.

A couple months later, Buffy invites you over again. Your kind pleas to meet at the local café are unsuccessful, but because she's someone you've known for a while, you decide to bear the beige one final time.

When you arrive, Buffy escorts you to her living room, but this time you sense something is different. Upon entering, you're struck with awe, and wonder if you've come to the same place. On the beige sofa rests a mix of floral and checked pillows, and a pretty handmade quilt drapes over its back. The once large, empty coffee table now displays a stack of books and magazines, and a wicker tray holds a pitcher of fresh yellow flowers, a bowl of green apples, and a small silver plate. The chair nearby now wears a knitted throw and a charming needlepoint pillow. The TV is still there, but somehow its prominence has lessened as it now blends seamlessly into the surroundings. And the barren walls? One now displays a set of botanical prints and the other, a lovely mirror. Lastly, you notice a cheerfully patterned area rug sitting on top of the beige wall-to-wall carpet in the seating area. You enjoy the same pleasant conversation over coffee, but this time you feel a flurry—the visit is more interesting and alive.

Through layering—ignited by the transforming ingredient of love—Buffy's living room went from boring to beautiful. As a result, your overall experience was more rich and satisfying. Now, you can't wait to return.

Similarly with cooking, each ingredient contributes its own personality to the aesthetics of the whole, and each element needs to be tended to with a nurturing heart. The secret lies in the approach. For example, when adding flour to the batter, do you dump it all in at once, or add it gradually, giving each addition time to assimilate? Do you add all the eggs and beat, or do you add and beat one at a time? If adding tomato paste, do you take the time to incorporate it into the rest of the sauce until combined well? Do you allow time for flavors to develop before adding the next item? When you stir, is it in a rushed, irregular fashion, or with gentle, even strokes? Do you skip—or skimp on—ingredients and expect the outcome to be the same? Each component in a recipe is pregnant with flavor and requires due time to flower. How we advance the process matters.

Tasting

Making a recipe is not always as straightforward as it seems. Any number of factors can influence the process, so it's critical that you "check in" frequently, and if necessary, be prepared to execute adjustments along the way.

There are many ways to check in during the cooking process—by viewing color (is it browned enough?), consistency (do I need to add more liquid?), texture (do I need to add a little more flour?), and smell (which I don't know anything about)—are just a few examples. But for me, the best way is to do a taste test. After all, isn't that what food is all about?

With sauces, I usually do a taste test when I'm about three-quarters of the way through a recipe. By then, enough time has evolved for the flavors to develop and to signal whether everything is on track for the final stretch of cooking. At this point, here are some questions I might ask myself: How does the food taste (obvious, but you'd be surprised)? Does it have enough "punch" (my code word for flavor)? If not, which ingredient can I add a little more of? Conversely, does it have too much punch? If so, how can I tone down the flavor?

When making adjustments, go slowly and stay disciplined. Start by adding a small amount of whichever ingredient. It's much easier to add, taste, and add a little more than to add too much all at once and find out that the overall flavor is disturbed. In that event, you're stuck having to backtrack and redesign the flavor. I've been there and it's no fun.

When the dish is done cooking and the burner gets turned off, pause a moment before serving it to family and friends. One critical task remains—conducting a final taste test. This could be a little slurp of sauce on a wooden spoon, or a dinky bite of Swiss chard, but regardless, now's when your dish can soar from good to marvelous. For example, you may discover some flavor got lost in the final phase of cooking—the sauce needs a dash more salt, the chili needs a little more oomph, or the green beans need a few more drops of lemon. That's why most of the instructions for the recipes contained in this cookbook finish by saying "Adjust to taste." Don't underestimate the value of this seemingly rudimentary direction. As the manager of the recipe, you determine the final level of flavor. Let it be, in Goldilocks's words, "Just right."

3. Be-Bold and Courageous

One day, I came across two opposing statistics from unrelated sources concerning America's food habits. One stated that less than 20 percent of people cook their meals at home.[2] The other said home cooks are running more than 10 million recipe searches per day on the Internet.[3] Assuming both to be true, I wondered what could account for the disparity between so many searches and actual home cooking? I figured lack of time to be one possibility. I also considered that for many, searching the Net for recipes is simply a fun and relaxing hobby. What's wrong with letting your imagination drift to a luscious and creamy baked custard, or a braised, tender roast? Besides, people collect everything from books to buttons, so why not recipes? But even these reasons didn't satisfy my curiosity. Then it occurred to me—the deeper reason is fear.

I understand this compulsion to STOP because I've been there myself. Fear paralyzes. It takes courage to try a new thing, even a simple recipe. We're creatures of habit and meandering even slightly away from our comfort zone—in this case, our regular weekly fare—is risky business. "Inspiration for another day," we mutter.

But wouldn't it be nice to operate in the kitchen with a little more chutzpah and plow through those fears with a little more pluck? Here are some tips that I've gleaned from my own experience that I hope will help you.

Tip# 1 - Dare to Try

Once you've found a new recipe that excites you, the first—and hardest—step is to decide to go for it. Here's where the battle is either won or lost. Nothing will ever happen without a decision; otherwise, you're not committed to taking action. Consider taking the leap! Daring to try will elevate your spirit from mundane to marvelous. The rest will follow naturally—making a list of ingredients you need to buy, taking out the pot or skillet, prepping the food, etc. So, muster all the gumption you've got, and go for it! I promise you'll be glad you did.

Tip #2 - Practice

The only way to achieve kitchen confidence is the old-fashioned way—one recipe at a time. Each recipe brings with it certain skills or techniques, like chopping or sautéing. And each produces its share of personal growth opportunities such as patience, tolerance of frustration, and acceptance. So, throughout a recipe you're learning on multiple levels. Naturally, the more you practice, the more comfortable you'll be, and the better you'll become.

Think of attaining kitchen confidence as climbing the rungs of a ladder where each rung represents a confidence builder. A novice will likely start at the lower rungs by preparing simpler recipes then gradually work up to more complicated ones. Alternatively, your cooking ability may already be half or three-quarters of the way up the ladder where you're pumping out fabulous feasts. Bravo! Whichever rung you're on, my advice is the same—keep going!

Now, there may be times when your ambition to take on more complicated recipes will exceed your location on the ladder. In these situations, I suggest following your heart. Regardless of the result, you'll either be happy you took the leap or know where to make the necessary adjustments next time. It'll be a win-win.

I've come to realize that food and cooking are multifaceted and inexhaustible fields, and there are always new and exciting things to learn. So, think of practice like cash—the more you do, the more you'll have in your back pocket.

Tip #3 - Manage Flops Wisely

While watching Julia Child on a cooking show one day, I saw her demonstrate the making of a soufflé. When the soufflé came out of the oven, its shape and color were just perfect. Then, when she turned it out from the mold onto the plate, this perfectly baked soufflé fell apart every which way. What I noticed, however, was not the fallen soufflé, but how composed Julia remained. She endured the disaster with her usual hearty chuckle and shifted the focus on how to avoid this kind of mistake in the future. Julia Child, the American dame of French cuisine, had a flop, yet turned it into her fortune.

Flops. We've all had them and know too well how discouraging they can be. The cookies burned, the meat overcooked, the sauce tasted bland. After all our gumption, expense, and hard work, there's nothing like a flop to drain the enthusiasm right out of you. Unfortunately, many home cooks give up at this point. To you I say, don't let one defeat deter you! Because we're human, flops are an inevitable part of cooking and merely signal that something needs to be done differently the next time.

Next time you experience a mishap, try to determine what went wrong. Sometimes the answer lies in the hardware—maybe you'll need to buy a certain kitchen tool, like a timer or a meat thermometer, or invest in higher quality cookware. Maybe you'll need to practice a certain technique a few more times, or juggle around the ingredients to achieve the desired taste. Many recipes take two or three attempts to get just right—with each attempt getting closer to the desired result. This is progress! Also consider the flop may have had nothing to do with your efforts, but instead, the recipe itself—there are plenty of faulty ones out there. Finally, once you've determined the problem and remedy, take your mind off the matter. Eventually, your enthusiasm and determination will start flowing again to try anew.

One day, while I was driving home listening to the radio, I caught the end of an interview with John Wooden, the beloved and esteemed former UCLA basketball coach and author of *Pyramid of Success*—a guidebook for success on the court and in life. The interviewer asked, "From all your life's experience, what's your one greatest piece of advice?"

Wooden, then in his nineties, replied, "Whether on the basketball court or in life, the greatest piece of advice I can give to anyone is that when things don't happen the way you want, keep your perspective. I've seen countless lives gone astray and opportunities lost because a person did not keep perspective."[4]

So, next time you experience a flop, keep calm, learn, maintain perspective, and press on toward your goal.

4. Be-In Charge

A recipe is like a roadmap. Both provide a sequence of instructions that explain how to get from Point A, your start, to Point B, your destination. For example, when driving somewhere for the first time you're likely to follow each turn and on-ramp exactly the way it's described in the directions. But after you've traveled there a few times and are familiar with the roads, you may decide to take an alternative route because it saves time or the scenery is more attractive. A recipe works in the same way. After a while, you may opt for deleting some of the ingredients specified and instead add your favorites. This demonstrates an important point—as the one behind the wheel (or in the kitchen), *you* are the one in charge, not a set of instructions.

Meet Betty, who loved nothing more than to cook by the book. She delighted in being told, ingredient-by-ingredient, step-by-step, what to do. For her, cooking was a no-brainer. Then one day her husband Bob turned to her and said, "Honey, I love you but your cooking is tasting bland and boring. Do you think you can do something to make it taste better?"

Betty, a dedicated rule follower, was beside herself. Until now, she had done everything correctly, measuring and following every letter to the tee. "Something has to change!" she exclaimed. So she got to work.

First, Betty started shopping differently by taking more time to explore unfamiliar produce and cuts of meat. Then she experimented with an array of herbs and spices, and even started eliminating some of the suggested ingredients and replacing them with some of her favorites. Betty was thrilled with her new discoveries and for the first time in her life she was having fun breaking the rules.

At dinner one evening, a couple months later, Bob turned to her and said, "Betty, this tastes delicious. What are you doing differently?"

Betty replied, "Thank you, sweetie, it's really not that mysterious. I finally learned how to bust through the bold print and be Betty."

This story reiterates that you—not a set of instructions—are in charge of a recipe. So give yourself permission to take certain liberties along the way, and be surprised by the results. In other words, if you love olives and want to add olives, add olives!

5. Be-Joyful

There's no greater joy and fulfillment for a cook than feeding a delicious and satisfying meal to family and friends. Sharing good home-cooked food creates a distinct and wonderful communal spirit. So always remember, you're not just nourishing empty stomachs, but also nurturing hearts and souls.

Cooking and feeding others is a ministry, whether it is just for one person or many. Take time to enjoy your cooking successes, and be gentle on yourself when things don't turn out exactly as you had hoped. Above all, pat yourself on the back for being organized, engaged, bold and courageous, and in charge. For in doing so, the gift of joy is yours to receive.

My mother and I at my girlfriend's wedding, 1983.

The Well-Stocked Pantry

Have you ever peeked in the next person's grocery cart while standing in the checkout line? One quick glance reveals distinct clues about their lifestyle and the foods they like to eat. The same is true of our pantries, and a well-stocked one is vital for any cook.

Why? A well-stocked pantry means most of the ingredients needed to prepare your wonderful dishes are always on hand. This eliminates extra trips to the store, and instead, permits you to focus on shopping for fresh, natural ingredients. For these reasons, I prefer to stock the pantry rather than overload the refrigerator.

The following ingredients are what you'll find in mine. They supply the building blocks for the recipes contained in this cookbook, can be purchased at your local supermarket, and are the soul of my Greek American kitchen.

Anchovies, fillets (2.5 ounce can)

Baking powder

Baking soda

Bay leaves

Butter, salted and unsalted (also called sweet butter)

Chili powder

Cheese, feta; sharp cheddar; Parmesan

Cinnamon, ground and sticks

Cloves, ground and whole

Eggs, grade AA large

Flour, all-purpose

Honey, orange clover

Legumes (such as lentils, beans, etc.)

Lemons

Nonstick cooking spray

Oil, extra virgin olive, canola, and vegetable

Olives, Mediterranean mix; Kalamata

Oregano, dried

Parsley, flat-leaf (Italian)

Pepper, whole peppercorns (for freshly ground)

Salt, coarse sea

Sesame seeds

Stock, chicken (or chicken broth)

Sugar, confectioners (powdered) and granulated

Thyme, fresh

Tomato paste (canned)

Tomato sauce (canned)

Tomatoes, whole peeled (canned)

Vanilla extract

Vinegar, red wine, white wine, or distilled

Walnuts

The Well-Equipped Kitchen

It goes without saying that any kind of pursuit requires the proper gear. Imagine the gardener without a trowel and hoe, the knitter without a pair of needles, or the sewer without a sewing machine—an otherwise comfortable and leisurely act becomes one of frustration and futility. And so it goes in the kitchen. Having the right equipment decreases labor, optimizes success, and makes you want to cook again and again.

While glossy food magazines will try to convince you that you need a sous vide, an egg-separating tool, or expensive bakeware, I believe equipping your kitchen with the basics is all you need to create delicious and satisfying food. Here, I've organized these essentials into four categories: *Appliances, Thermometers, Hardware,* and *Accessories.*

Appliances

There are two workhorses on my countertop I can't do without. One is a full-size **food processor** and the other is a **freestanding electric mixer.** If you don't already own these, you may want to consider buying or saving up for them—both are substantial time and energy savers. For example, if the recipe says, "beat for 20 minutes," envision yourself changing the laundry and grabbing the mail while your electric mixer is doing the work. Or, if it reads, "2 onions, finely chopped," picture the tedious job completed at the flick of a switch. Besides, both these appliances are user friendly, and each comes with its own separate attachments (the food processor with a kneader, shredder, and slicer, and the freestanding mixer with a whisk and dough hook). You won't regret the investment.

Thermometers

After we remodeled our kitchen and bought new appliances, I couldn't understand why our food cooked so fast in the oven and sometimes even burned. On a whim, I went to the hardware store and bought an **oven thermometer** only to discover my new designer oven ran thirty-five degrees hotter than what the setting indicated. Unfortunately, this is a common problem and will cause all your time, energy, and expense to literally go up in smoke. Even 5 to 10 degrees can make a difference. Investing in an inexpensive oven thermometer eliminates this problem.

In addition to an oven thermometer, I highly recommend a **meat** or an **instant-read** thermometer. Unless you're a good guesser, or enjoy cutting slits into your roast until it looks like chopped beef, it's impossible to know if it's done to your liking without inserting a thermometer inside before it goes into the oven.

Hardware

In my kitchen, these items do the heavy lifting:

Baking sheets

Baking pans (small, medium, large, and extra large)

Broiling pan (large)

Covered deep skillet (13 x 3-inch)

Knife sharpener and knives (boning, paring, serrated, utility, etc.)

Loaf pans (standard size)

Mixing bowls (2 sets each of small, medium, and large, plus 1 extra large)

Roasting pans (medium and large)

Saucepans with lids (small, medium, large, and extra large)

Skillets, nonstick (small, medium, and large)

Stockpot (20 to 25-quart)

Accessories

These smaller items are just as important:

Cooling rack

Fat separator

Immersion blender

Measuring cups (one set for wet ingredients and another for dry)

Measuring spoons

Mixer, portable electric

Nut chopper

Paper baking cups

Parchment paper

Pastry brushes (1- and 2-inch wide)   **Steamer insert**

Roasting rack   **Tongs**

Sifter   **Whisk**

Now, let's get cooking!

Recipes and Tales

Appetizers

Baby Meatballs
Keftedakia

I'll never forget the day my *yiayia* (grandmother)—demure in her black skirt and low-heeled pumps—climbed over our backyard fence to pick some mint for the Greek meatballs she was going to prepare for dinner that night. What a testimony to cooking with fresh, natural ingredients!

In their smaller form, these meatballs make a hearty appetizer and are ideal for cocktail buffets—people seem to gravitate toward them. Plus, their minty flavor bursts with pleasant surprise.

Makes 50

Meatballs

1 pound lean ground beef

2 slices white bread (for soft breadcrumbs), or ½ cup dried breadcrumbs

2 eggs, lightly beaten

1 small onion, grated or processed in a food processor for 20 seconds

1 clove garlic, finely chopped

2 tablespoons milk

1 tablespoon olive oil

6 fresh mint leaves, finely chopped (about 1 ½ teaspoons)

½ teaspoon dried oregano

1 ½ teaspoons salt

Dash freshly ground black pepper

¾ cup flour

1 cup vegetable oil

Paper towels

Toothpicks

Dipping Sauce (optional)

¼ cup ketchup

¼ cup chili sauce

Few drops of lemon juice

For the Meatballs: Place the meat in a medium bowl. To make soft breadcrumbs, remove crust from bread slices and place in a food processor. Process for 10 seconds and add to meat. *Or,* if using prepared dried breadcrumbs, add to meat. Add eggs, onion, garlic, milk, olive oil, mint, dried oregano, salt, and pepper to mixture and mix by hand until combined well.

Place flour in a shallow bowl and set near the stove. Pour vegetable oil into a large (13 x 2½-inch) deep fry skillet and cook on medium high heat until oil starts to sizzle. Meanwhile, pour a little olive oil in the palms of your hands and rub together. In batches (you'll need to make 2 or 3), scoop out a heaping teaspoon of the meat mixture and roll into a ball with the palms of your hands. Coat meatballs lightly with flour and place in hot skillet. Reduce to medium heat and cook for 6-7 minutes, turning a couple times with a slotted spoon to brown on all sides. Drain on paper towels. Transfer to a serving platter and serve warm with toothpicks and dipping sauce (optional).

For the Dipping Sauce: Stir ketchup, chili sauce, and lemon juice together in a small bowl; stir. Serve alongside warm meatballs.

Hot Baked Crabmeat Special

When something comes along that captures your attention—like a smart outfit or pretty pair of shoes—don't be afraid to get more information. Ask and you will receive. Ask and it shall be given to you. Seek and you will find. That's how I ended up with this recipe.

I was in Baltimore for a work seminar, and one night our class was invited to our professor's home for dinner. When we arrived, the hostess—the lovely Mrs. Olson—served this hot crabmeat appetizer. Needless to say, I was smitten after the first bite.

"May I please have your recipe?" I asked.

"Of course, it's so easy," she replied while writing out the ingredients from memory. Since then I've made it hundreds of times, and it always goes quickly—especially when paired with buttery, flaky croissant-type crackers.

All these years later, I still think of Mrs. Olson and how her small, generous act continues to bless many. And to think, it all started with a simple question.

Serves 8 to 10

9 ounces fresh crabmeat

1 (8-ounce) package regular or low-fat cream cheese

2 fresh green onions (scallions), finely sliced

½ cup mayonnaise

Dash paprika

Preheat oven to 350 degrees. Place crabmeat in a medium bowl and separate larger pieces with a fork. Soften cream cheese in the microwave for 20-30 seconds and add to bowl. Add green onions and mayonnaise, and stir with a spatula to combine well. Turn mixture into a 9 x 9-inch baking pan and wipe smooth. Add a dash paprika and place in preheated oven. Cook about 18-20 minutes, or until bubbly. Remove and let cool about five minutes. Serve hot with crackers.

Easy Olive Marinade
Marinada Elias

Despite our roaming the sizzling streets of Athens the summer of 1975, you could always count on my cousin Angela and I showing up at her home precisely at 1:00 p.m. for lunch. Needless to say, her mother, *Thia* (Aunt) Ellie was a fabulous cook.

When *Thio* (Uncle) Yianni arrived after closing his shop for the feverish afternoon as was customary, we all headed outside on their balcony to sit around a beautifully set table draped with a floral cloth. Then from the kitchen, *Thia* Ellie would carry out the fruit of her morning's labor—stuffed tomatoes or fried potatoes, baked chicken and vegetables, Greek salad, fresh country bread, and small dishes containing cheese and olives. I always appreciated her hospitality.

Of course, this warm, generous attitude toward guests and strangers, or *filoxenia* (hospitality), isn't anything new to Greek culture. Rather, it's a hallmark feature. "*Fai, fai* (Eat, eat)," they say while offering food and drink ensuring a guest is well cared for.

To assure the same experience for your visitors, why not consider starting off with the essence of the Mediterranean, the meaty and nutritious olive? Most enjoy munching on at least a few while sipping their favorite libation, plus they leave plenty of room for the meal to come.

When it comes to Greek olives, each kind is unique depending on where it's sourced. For instance, in Crete you'll find the baby green ones; on the Chalkidiki peninsula in northern Greece, the larger green types; in Kalamata—located on the Peloponnese peninsula in southern Greece—the popular black kind that bears its name; and on the island of Thassos, the dark, wrinkly, and slightly bitter variety. But if you're having trouble deciding, why not select a medley?

This simple marinade recipe lends flavor to olives aside from their usual brined liquid. For extra kick, consider adding one clove of finely chopped garlic.

Serves 6

1 ½ cups Greek or Mediterranean olives (about ½ pound)

3 tablespoons extra virgin olive oil

1 ½ tablespoons red wine vinegar

½ teaspoon dried oregano

½ teaspoon salt

Dash freshly ground black pepper

½ teaspoon finely chopped flat-leaf parsley (optional)

Drain olives and place in a bowl. Add olive oil, vinegar, oregano, salt and pepper, and mix until combined well; adjust to taste. Refrigerate until ready to serve. Add parsley and serve. *(Note: Remove from refrigerator at least 15 minutes before serving for the fat to liquefy.)*

The Freshest Tortilla Dip

Some occasions ooze with festivity.

Take the time our Gourmet Club celebrated German Night, for example. We knew we were in for a fun time when the hostess answered the door wearing a dirndl dress, white tights, and black patent flats. To add to the gaiety, steady accordion rhythms from polka music blared merrily in the background. In no time—and with beer-filled steins—we were all rollicking with laughter. Somehow, the Bratwurst and Muenster Cheese on Pumpernickel appetizers, and Marinated Sauerbraten with Red Cabbage along with Hot Potato Salad for the entrée played second fiddle to the jolly spirit permeating the room. Even the delicious German Chocolate Torte met a quiet hush compared to the hilarity happening.

Reminiscent of good cheer is my friend Lori Farley's Freshest Tortilla Dip. A gourmet cook, she brought this attractive and colorfully layered dip to our kids' soccer party one year, and I was instantly taken. Fortunately for me (and now, you) she generously shared her recipe.

For bigger crowds, I've seen the ingredients doubled and even tripled, and the platter just gets larger and the mound higher. Teamed with margaritas, it makes for a festive starter or even a light supper. So toast up! To friends and fun!

Serves 6 to 8

Meat Layer

½ **pound ground beef**

1½ **tablespoons extra virgin olive oil**

2 **cloves garlic, finely chopped**

1 **small onion, finely chopped**

1 **(1.25-ounce) package taco seasoning**

½ **cup water**

1 **(15-ounce) can pinto beans, drained well**

1 **(8-ounce) can tomato sauce**

2 **teaspoons chili powder**

1 **teaspoon dried oregano**

1 **teaspoon ground cumin**

½ **teaspoon crushed red pepper or freshly ground black pepper**

¼ **teaspoon salt**

Other Layers

1 **cup cherry tomatoes, sliced in half**

3 **fresh green onions (scallions), finely sliced**

2 **medium avocados, diced**

½ **cup loosely packed cilantro leaves, finely chopped**

2 **cups grated cheddar cheese**

1 **(16-ounce) container salsa**

1 (8-ounce) container sour cream*

1 (8-ounce) container thick Greek-style plain yogurt*

1 large (16-ounce) bag tortilla chips

(*Note: You can substitute the sour cream and yogurt with 1 (16-ounce) container of regular or reduced-fat sour cream.)

Advance Preparation: Drain the yogurt. Line a strainer with fine mesh cheesecloth or a tea towel and place the strainer over a bowl. Add the yogurt and cover. Place in the refrigerator for a couple hours; discard liquid.

For the Meat: Place olive oil, garlic, and onion in a medium (3-quart) saucepan and cook on medium heat until soft, about 2-3 minutes, stirring occasionally.

Break up the meat into small pieces and add to the pot. Brown and drain fat.

Add taco seasoning and water; stir. Cook on medium heat until liquid evaporates, stirring occasionally.

Add drained pinto beans, tomato sauce, chili powder, dried oregano, ground cumin, salt, and pepper; stir until combined well. Cook over medium heat for 5 minutes, stirring occasionally.

Pour meat mixture onto a heatproof platter and spread into a thin, even layer. Let cool to room temperature for about 30-35 minutes.

For the Other Layers: Drain salsa thoroughly in a colander. Set aside the tomatoes, green onions, diced avocados, cilantro, and cheese.

After the meat layer has cooled, stir together the sour cream and drained yogurt until combined well. Spread the mixture evenly over the meat with a spatula.

Add the cheese, distributing evenly. In the following order, add the drained salsa, avocados, green onions, cilantro, and tomatoes, also distributing evenly. Refrigerate until ready to serve. Serve alongside a bowl of tortilla chips.

Herbed Clam Dip

I enjoyed this dip during my childhood, and to bring it into the twenty-first century, I've added fresh herbs. Otherwise, the lemon adds just the right pizzazz.

This dip is ideal on game day in front of the TV, and if your home is like mine, it'll be devoured before the final score.

Makes about 1 ½ cups

1 (8-ounce) package regular or low-fat cream cheese

1 (6.5-ounce) can chopped clams, 2 tablespoons juice reserved

2 tablespoons lemon juice (about 1 medium lemon)

½ teaspoon Worcestershire sauce

1 teaspoon finely chopped flat-leaf (Italian) parsley

1 teaspoon finely chopped fresh tarragon

1 large (14-ounce) bag potato chips

Soften the cream cheese in the microwave for 20-30 seconds and place in a medium bowl; stir with a wooden spoon until the consistency is smooth and creamy.

Reserve 2 tablespoons clam juice; set aside. Drain clams in a colander.

Add drained clams, reserved clam juice, lemon juice, Worcestershire sauce, parsley, and tarragon to cream cheese and stir until combined well. Adjust to taste. Pour into a serving bowl and serve alongside a large bowl of potato chips.

A Special Guacamole Dip

A friend introduced me to this recipe many years ago and I've been making it ever since. It may require a little more work than you're accustomed, but the combination of ingredients gives this popular dip a complexity and flavor all its own. The secret ingredient? Lemon.

Makes about 3 cups

2 medium to large avocados, halved and pitted

2 tablespoons mayonnaise

2 tablespoons plus 1 teaspoon lemon juice (about 1 lemon)

2 tablespoons chili sauce

¾ teaspoon Worcestershire sauce

½ teaspoon hot pepper sauce

Dash freshly ground black pepper

¼ medium onion, coarsely chopped

1 small tomato, cored, seeded, and coarsely chopped

1 large (16-ounce) bag tortilla chips

Scoop out avocado pulp, place in a medium bowl, and mash.

Add mayonnaise, lemon juice, chili sauce, Worcestershire sauce, hot pepper sauce, and pepper. Stir until combined well.

Add onion and stir. Cover with plastic wrap and refrigerate until ready to serve. Add chopped tomatoes; stir. Pour dip in a small bowl and serve alongside tortilla chips.

Phyllo-Wrapped Cheese Triangles
Tiropites

Do you remember that special place from your childhood? My mother referred to hers often—the seaside village of Vouliagmeni, about twenty-five minutes south of Athens.

Today, Vouliagmeni is considered the Riviera of Greece and commands some of the highest real estate prices in all of Europe. It's easy to understand why—this picturesque community nestled in the foothills of the Hymettus Mountains borders the beautiful, lapis waters of the Aegean Sea. But in those days, it was desolate beach and undeveloped land—the end of the road.

Of her childhood my mother used to say, "Every June when school got out, my mother rented a home in Vouliagmeni for the whole summer, and my father came to visit when he could get away from work. My sisters, brothers, and I got black from being out on the beach all day. Sometimes, *Kirios Vasili* (Mr. Basil) would take us out on his *varka* (boat) for a ride. Our lives were so healthy and innocent; we had no worries."

Years later, when I visited Greece for the first time as a ten-year old with my mother and brother, she brought us to that same beach from her childhood. But in addition to sand and shore, I experienced some pleasures of another sort—tasty food. For example, after my brother and I dried off from a swim and moaned about how hungry we were, my mother would appear a few minutes later with fresh poor-boy rolls lined with sweet butter containing a few slices of mortadella and a thick chunk of feta cheese. Or, she would bring us giant *tiropites* (cheese triangles), which I savored for their salty bite. These flavors were familiar from back home, but somehow in situ my senses came alive.

My mother enjoyed making the smaller version of these cheese triangles as appetizers, especially on Thanksgiving, where they got gobbled up in a hurry. It's no surprise—they're light, tasty, and fun to eat. Besides, they freeze beautifully—an asset for a busy host.

Makes 40 triangles

Filling

¾ **pound feta cheese, drained and grated**

8 ounces regular or 4% small curd cottage cheese

8 ounces ricotta cheese

4 ounces regular or light cream cheese

3 eggs

1 tablespoon finely chopped flat-leaf (Italian) parsley

½ **teaspoon salt**

<u>Remaining Ingredients</u>

1 cup (2 sticks) butter

1 pound #4 (fine) phyllo

2 tablespoons milk

Read Appendix A, *Being At Ease with Phyllo* (see page 321).

For the Filling: Soften cream cheese for 20-30 seconds in the microwave and place in a medium bowl. Add feta, cottage, and ricotta cheeses.

In a separate bowl, beat eggs lightly with a fork. Add to cheese mixture.

Add parsley and salt; stir with a wood spoon until mixture is combined thoroughly. Cover with plastic and refrigerate about 45 minutes to 1 hour.

For the Remainder: Preheat oven to 350 degrees.

Melt butter in a small saucepan. Grease 2 (15 x 10 x 1-inch) baking sheets with melted butter; set aside. Place milk in a small bowl; set aside.

Take one sheet of phyllo and place on a cutting board with the long side facing you. Wipe sheet with melted butter using a 2-inch-wide pastry brush. Take a second sheet and place it on top of the first one and wipe also with butter.

Cut phyllo vertically into 3½-inch-wide strips. Place 2 full teaspoons of filling a half-inch from the bottom of each strip. Roll each strip like a flag as follows: Starting with the lower right corner (or, if you're left-handed, with the lower left corner), lift corner to the opposite side and continue rolling toward opposite sides until you've reached the end. Dip your index finger in the milk and press the edge down to seal.

Place triangles on the prepared baking sheet and brush the tops with melted butter. Repeat the above with the remaining filling. Place baking sheets in preheated oven and cook for 15 minutes, or until light golden. Transfer to a serving dish with a spatula and serve hot. *(Note: To freeze, cover uncooked cheese triangles on baking sheets with aluminum foil, or place in an airtight container; store in freezer. When ready to cook, preheat oven to 350 degrees. Uncover and cook for 20 minutes, or until light golden.)*

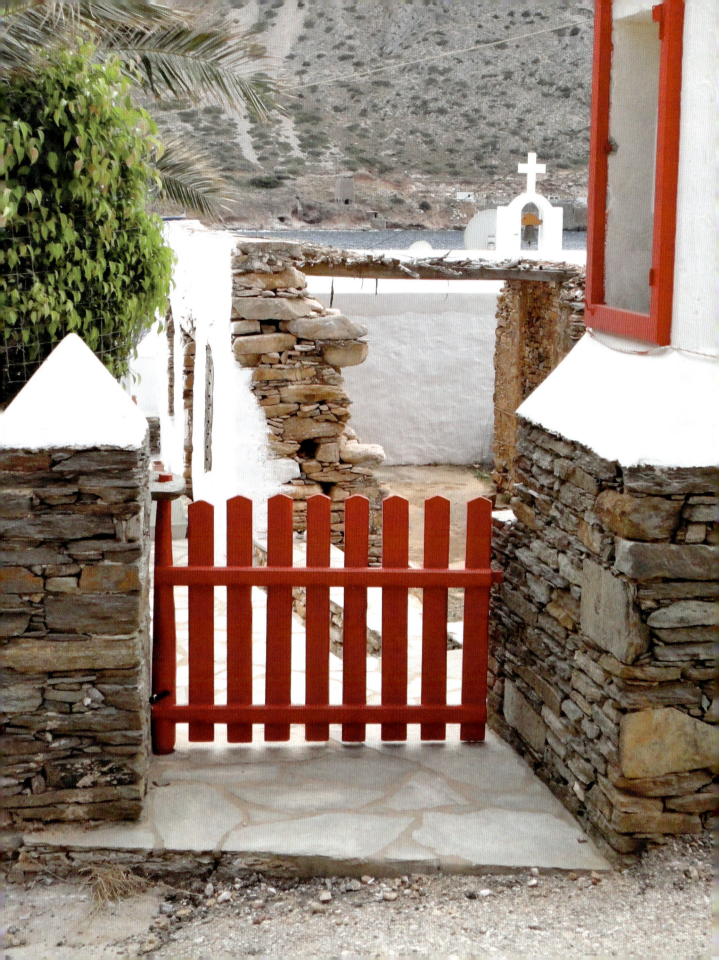

Cheese and Olive Spread on Rye

There are certain perils associated with Appetizer Duty. One is arriving late. (Just imagine the host[ess] and guests with nothing to nibble on until you show up—an hour late.) Another is transporting them. For instance, if your appetizers aren't safely secured in the car, a sudden stop may render them scattered all over the floor. Unfortunately, for our Gourmet Club's French-themed kick-off dinner, both injuries occurred.

Luckily, after some nifty reconstruction, the hors d'oeuvres were salvaged. By the end of the evening, these mishaps were but a distant memory—largely due to the Seafood Crepes and Crème Caramel that melted in our mouths, and the merriment we enjoyed.

Barring these hazards, serving finger food is like hanging a large welcome sign, and I can't think of a more tasty reception than my mother's Cheese and Olive Spread on Rye. It's ideal for parties ranging from a few to fifty—just double, triple, or quadruple the ingredients for larger gatherings. And, don't worry about having leftovers; these get gulped down in a hurry.

If you're not fond of rye, sliced sourdough works equally well. But regardless, be sure the bread is very fresh.

Serves 4 to 6

8 slices (½ pound) rye bread

2 cups grated cheddar cheese

1 (4.25-ounce) can of chopped olives, drained

½ cup regular or low-fat mayonnaise

2 fresh green onions (scallions), finely chopped

1 teaspoon chili powder

Line a (15 x 10 x 1-inch) baking sheet with aluminum foil; set aside.

Place the cheese, olives, mayonnaise, green onions, and chili powder in a medium bowl; stir with a wooden spoon combined well.

Position oven rack to the third level from the top, and preheat to the broiler setting.

Spread cheese mixture onto each slice of bread, covering it completely. With a sharp knife, cut each slice into halves or quarters, depending on your preference, and place on prepared pan. Place pan in the preheated oven for about 1-2 minutes, or until cheese is bubbly. Transfer to a platter and serve hot.

Ramos Fizz

Also called Gin Fizz, my father used to make this sweet, frothy beverage every Christmas morning after we opened our gifts. To add to the celebratory mood, he would serve it in champagne flutes. As a child, I somehow managed to sneak in a sip here or there, but eventually the time came when I could enjoy my very own.

Of course, you don't need to wait for the holidays to make Ramos Fizz. It makes an excellent late morning or midday libation. But in our home, we reserve this special drink for our Christmas morning tradition—only now my husband and I enjoy it with our adult children. But first, we make a toast in memory of their beloved *papou* (grandfather). Somewhere, I know he's smiling.

Serves 4 to 6

⅓ cup plus 3 tablespoons gin

⅓ cup plus 2 tablespoons half-and-half

4 heaping tablespoons crushed pineapple

1 egg

4 tablespoons sugar

Dash lemon juice

8 ice cubes

Pour gin and half-and-half into a blender. Add 4 heaping tablespoons crushed pineapple. Add egg, sugar, lemon juice, and ice cubes. Blend for 30 seconds. Adjust to taste and pour.

Soups

Chicken Stock

Besides its unparalleled flavor, there's something about making stock that's deeply nurturing and satisfying.

From experimenting, I discovered using 2 small roasting chickens yields enough drippings from the bones and tendons for the stock to congeal—a sign of success! Also, I usually make this recipe one day before I make the soup because I find it much easier to scrape off the top layer of fat once it's had a chance to solidify overnight in the refrigerator.

After scraping the fat, just warm the congealed stock on low heat until it liquefies, and you're ready to go forward with your soup recipe. Also, consider freezing the stock for when the whim strikes. What a welcome thought to know a homemade batch is awaiting you.

Makes about 2½ quarts

2 (3 to 3½-pound) roasting chickens

1 large onion, peeled and quartered

3 whole cloves garlic, peeled

2 medium leeks

2 medium carrots, peeled

2 medium ribs celery, rinsed

4 sprigs fresh thyme

4 sprigs flat-leaf (Italian) parsley

2 bay leaves

1 tablespoon salt

Water

Trim excess fat from chickens. Rinse and place in an extra-large (20-25 quart) stockpot, or the largest pot you have on hand. Add onion and garlic.

Trim the root end from the leeks and trim the darker green leaves; discard. Clean leeks by making a lengthwise slit and fanning the leaves open under running water to remove dirt. Slice in half crosswise; add to pot.

Slice carrots and celery in half crosswise; add to pot. Add thyme, parsley, bay leaves, and salt. Add water so that contents are submerged and the water level is about 1 inch from the rim. Bring to a boil. Reduce to medium heat and skim the scum as needed. Cook, uncovered, for 3 hours adding about 3-4 cups of water halfway through the cooking time.

When cooking is done, remove larger pieces with tongs, allowing the precious stock to drain off into the pot first; discard. Position a fine mesh strainer or colander over a large (5-quart) saucepan and strain remaining contents; discard. Cover with lid and place in the refrigerator to let stand overnight. The next day, scrape off the top layer of fat with a spoon; discard. Heat on low for stock to liquefy. Measure the amount needed for your soup recipe, and use or freeze the rest for another occasion. *Or,* if using the stock right away, degrease in batches using a fat separator. Measure the amount needed for your soup recipe and proceed.

Chicken Noodle Soup
Kotopoulo Manestra Soupa

Now and then we all reach inside the cupboard for a can of soup—it's just so convenient. But as my mother used to say, "There's nothing like homemade," and I agree. Here, chunky pieces of meat, fresh vegetables, and a savory broth characterize my version of America's most popular and comforting soup. Additionally, it pairs well with The Best Sourdough Croutons (see page 115). So although the canned variety is just an aisle away, don't be surprised if after trying this your inclinations sway.

Makes about 5 quarts

1 pound cooked chicken breast meat, or 2 large uncooked boneless, skinless chicken breasts*

4 ounces dried extra wide noodles

1 tablespoon extra virgin olive oil

Salt and freshly ground black pepper

⅓ cup extra virgin olive oil

½ medium onion, finely chopped

2 medium carrots, peeled and finely chopped

2 medium ribs celery, finely chopped

2 quarts Chicken Stock (see page 64), or chicken broth

1 bay leaf

½ cup loosely packed flat-leaf (Italian) parsley, finely chopped

3 tablespoons lemon juice (about 1 ½ lemons)

(*Note: Some stores carry packaged precooked chicken breast meat. Alternatively, you can buy a cooked roasted chicken and remove the breasts, reserving the other parts for another occasion. Otherwise, steam 2 large boneless, skinless chicken breasts. To do this, insert a steam basket inside a saucepan and add water until it reaches the bottom of the basket. Add chicken breasts and bring to a boil. Cook, covered, for 8 to 10 minutes. Turn over and cook for another 8 to 10 minutes, or until a slit into the thickest part of the breast is white and not raw.)

Cut cooked chicken into bite-size pieces; set aside.

Cook noodles according to package directions; drain. Place noodles back in pot and add 1 tablespoon olive oil and ½ teaspoon salt; stir and set aside.

Pour ⅓ cup olive oil into a large (5-quart) saucepan. Add onion, carrots, celery, bay leaf, 1 teaspoon salt, and dash pepper. Stir until combined well and cook on medium heat for 6-8 minutes, stirring occasionally.

Add chicken stock and bring to a boil. Reduce heat to medium and cook for 5 minutes, partially covered, for flavors to develop. Remove pot from burner and add cooked chicken, cooked noodles, parsley, lemon juice, 1 teaspoon salt, and dash pepper; stir. *(Note: If soup is too thick, add ½ cup water at a time until you reach desired consistency.)* Adjust to taste. Discard bay leaf and serve hot.

Bean Soup
Fassoulada

When the time came that my mother could no longer live alone, my family and I welcomed her into our home. Though her health was declining, she still enjoyed life, and our relationship continued to provide us both with deep pleasure. In the late afternoon, she would sit in a comfortable chair in the corner of our kitchen, sip a glass of wine, and watch me prepare dinner.

One day, feeble yet determined, she got up and walked over to the stove to see what I had made. "Oh, Bean Soup!" she said. And, in the same breath added, "It's not done yet."

"What do you mean it's not done? How can you tell?" I asked.

"I can just tell by looking at it," my mother answered.

And she was right. The deep, rich hues that appear around the rim of the pot signaling doneness hadn't yet appeared, so back on the stove it went. Feeble, yes, but her kitchen instincts prevailed.

The humble legume carries a proud role in Greek cuisine—particularly when it comes to soup. In Greece, Bean Soup is so endeared it may well be considered a national treasure. Every child grows up fondly remembering his or her family's rendition. This is ours.

Adding a little vinegar in the end—a popular ingredient for Greek soups—imparts the final depth of flavor. Just make sure when enjoying a bowl that there's some fresh country bread nearby—no one escapes this meal without dunking and dousing a slice inside its savory broth.

Serves 8

1 pound dry white beans, such as cannellini or Great Northern

½ cup extra virgin olive oil

2-3 cloves garlic, finely chopped

1 medium onion, finely chopped

2 medium carrots, peeled and finely chopped

2 medium ribs celery, finely chopped

½ cup loosely packed flat-leaf (Italian) parsley, finely chopped

Salt and freshly ground black pepper

1 (28-ounce) can whole peeled tomatoes, or 2 (11.5-ounce) cans tomato juice

2 quarts Chicken Stock (see page 64), or chicken broth

1 teaspoon ground cinnamon

2 bay leaves

1 teaspoon sugar

1 tablespoon red wine vinegar

Advance Preparation: Pour beans into a large bowl and cover with water. Let soak overnight. Drain in a colander; set aside.

Pour olive oil into a large (5-quart) saucepan and add garlic and onions. Cook on medium heat until soft, about 2-3 minutes, stirring occasionally. Add carrots, celery, parsley, ½ teaspoon salt and dash pepper, and cook for a few minutes until vegetables soften, stirring occasionally.

Process the whole tomatoes in a food processor for 10 seconds and add to the pot. *Or,* if using tomato juice, add to the pot. Add chicken stock and stir until combined well. Add drained beans, stir, and bring to a boil. Reduce heat to medium low and add 1 teaspoon salt, dash pepper, cinnamon, bay leaves, and sugar. Stir until combined well and cook, partially covered, for 1½ to 2 hours, or until beans are tender, stirring occasionally. *(Note: If soup is too thick, add water ½ cup at a time, until you reach the desired consistency.)* Remove from burner and add vinegar; stir. Adjust to taste and serve hot.

Lentil Soup
Fakes Soupa

I've made this healthy, traditional Greek soup so many times I'm certain I could do it with my eyes closed. But when the time came to writing out the recipe for this cookbook, I sure had a tough time trying to decipher my scribbled notes from the backside of an old envelope from when I observed my mother make it during my college days!

Hopefully, my recipe-writing skills have evolved since then, but rest assured—the formula remains the same.

Makes about 4 ½ quarts

1 pound dry lentils

⅓ cup extra virgin olive oil

1 medium onion, finely chopped

2 medium cloves garlic, peeled and finely chopped

2 medium celery ribs, finely chopped

2 medium carrots, finely chopped

Salt and freshly ground black pepper

2 quarts Chicken Stock (see page 64), or chicken broth

2 (11.5-ounce) cans tomato juice

2 bay leaves

1 teaspoon cinnamon

1 ½ cups water, plus a little extra if needed

2 tablespoons red wine vinegar

Rinse lentils in a colander and drain; set aside. Pour olive oil into a large (5-quart) saucepan and add onion, garlic, celery, carrots, 1 teaspoon salt, and dash pepper. Stir together and cook on medium heat until vegetables are soft, about 5 minutes, stirring occasionally.

Add stock or broth and bring to a boil. Add drained lentils, tomato juice, bay leaves, cinnamon, 1 teaspoon salt, and dash pepper. Stir until combined well and return to a boil. Reduce heat to medium-low and cook, partially covered, for 35 minutes. After 35 minutes, add 1 ½ cups water and ½ teaspoon salt; stir. Cook another 25 minutes partially covered, stirring occasionally. *(Note: If the soup is too thick, add ½ cup water at a time until you achieve desired consistency.)* Remove from burner and add vinegar; stir. Adjust to taste. Discard bay leaves and serve hot.

Potato Leek Soup

I must confess I'm not a huge fan of cream soups, but I never passed up my mother's Potato Leek. Her flavorful rendition uses simple, classic ingredients. The best part is it only takes about an hour to prepare from start to finish. I really think using homemade chicken stock makes a difference, but the store-bought version also works well. Otherwise, a green salad complements this meal nicely.

Makes about 4 quarts

5 russet potatoes (2½ to 3 pounds), peeled and rinsed

Salt

¼ cup (half a stick) butter

1 medium onion, finely chopped

3 medium leeks, white part only

3 medium ribs celery, finely chopped

1 chicken bouillon cube, roughly chopped

1 quart (4 cups) Chicken Stock (see page 64), or chicken broth

1½ cups half-and-half

1½ cups low-fat (2%) milk

2 teaspoons finely chopped flat-leaf (Italian) parsley for garnish (optional)

Place potatoes in a large pot and cover with water. Add 2 teaspoons salt and bring to a boil. Cook until tender or can easily be pierced with a fork. Drain in a colander; set aside.

Trim the root end and green leaves from leeks; discard. To clean the remaining white part, make a lengthwise slit and fan open under running water; pat dry with paper towels. Slice each leek lengthwise into quarters, then slice crosswise into ½-inch widths; set aside.

Place butter and onion in the same pot used for the potatoes and cook on medium heat until the onions are soft, about 2-3 minutes, stirring occasionally. Add celery, leeks, chicken bouillon, and 1 teaspoon salt. Stir until combined well and cook for 5 minutes, stirring occasionally. Add chicken stock, stir, and bring to a boil. Reduce to medium heat and cook, uncovered, for 10 minutes.

Remove pot from burner.

Add cooked potatoes and ½ teaspoon salt. With an immersion blender, blend mixture just until the potatoes are mashed. Gradually add the half-and-half and milk and blend until the mixture is completely smooth and uniform. *(Note: If using a standard blender or food processor instead of an immersion blender, transfer the mixture in batches and process until completely smooth; transfer back to pot.)* If soup is too thick, add a dash of milk a little at a time until you achieve the desired consistency. Adjust to taste. Heat on medium until hot, but not boiling. Garnish with chopped parsley, if desired, and serve

Fresh Tomato Soup
Domatosoupa

My *Thia* (Aunt) Ellie was a dedicated home cook, and luckily, I dined at her home in Athens many times that summer between high school and college. Once, I peeked inside her refrigerator and noticed it was practically empty! I wondered how could so much delicious food come out of an empty refrigerator? On another occasion, I caught a glimpse of *Thia* standing by her sink lathering and scrubbing large, plump tomatoes with soap. I later realized that in Greece, shopping daily for fresh food was de rigueur and the pesticide-free movement already thriving.

Whether you lather your own or just do a quick rinse job, tomatoes constitute the main element for this traditional Greek soup. Accompanied with baby-teeth-like pasta, called *kirtharaki* or *manestra* (orzo), it makes a light and satisfying meal, especially in late summer when these scarlet sweethearts are in peak season.

Serves 6

4 to 4½ pounds vine-ripe plum tomatoes

¼ cup extra virgin olive oil

1 medium sweet onion (also called Vidalia, WallaWalla, or Maui), finely chopped

2 medium cloves garlic, finely chopped

Salt and freshly ground black pepper

2 tablespoons tomato paste

2 quarts Chicken Stock (see page 64), or chicken broth

1 teaspoon ground cinnamon

1 tablespoon sugar

½ cup uncooked orzo

2 teaspoons finely chopped flat-leaf (Italian) parsley (optional, for garnish)

Skin, core, and seed the tomatoes. Strain and reserve the juice. Coarsely chop the tomatoes and place in a medium bowl. Add reserved juice; set aside.

Place olive oil in a large (5-quart) saucepan and add onion, garlic, 1 teaspoon salt, and dash pepper; stir until combined well. Cook on medium heat 2-3 minutes or until soft, stirring occasionally.

Add chopped tomatoes and reserved juice to onion mixture; stir to combine well. Add tomato paste and incorporate into the mixture.

Add chicken stock, cinnamon, sugar, ½ teaspoon salt, and dash pepper; stir to combine well. Bring to a boil. Reduce to medium heat and cook for 15 minutes, uncovered. Add orzo and cook, uncovered, for another 10 minutes, or until al dente; stir occasionally. Adjust to taste. Serve hot, adding chopped parsley over each serving, if desired.

Vegetable Soup
Soupa Lachaniko

The key to this recipe is making sure the vegetables are cleaned, chopped, and placed near the stove *before* you start to cook. Many of them can even be prepared the night before, covered with plastic wrap, and stored in the refrigerator so they're ready to go when you arrive home from work. After thirty or forty minutes of cooking time, a tasty and nutritious meal will be yours to enjoy.

Serves 6

3 medium russet potatoes (about 1 ½ pounds), peeled

½ pound green beans

1 medium zucchini

⅓ cup extra virgin olive oil

1 medium onion, finely chopped

3 medium cloves garlic, finely chopped

2 medium carrots, peeled and finely chopped

2 medium ribs celery, finely chopped

1 cup loosely packed flat-leaf (Italian) parsley, finely chopped

Salt and freshly ground black pepper

2 quarts Chicken Stock (see page 64), or chicken broth

½ cup frozen peas

1 (28-ounce) can diced tomatoes

1 (11.5-ounce) can tomato juice

1 tablespoon sugar

Cover potatoes with water in a large (5-quart) saucepan and bring to a boil. Cook 10-12 minutes. Transfer to a plate and let cool 10 minutes.

On a cutting board, slice potatoes in half lengthwise. With the flat side facing down, cut the potatoes into quarters, then eighths. Cut crosswise into ½-inch widths; set aside on a plate.

Trim endpoints from green beans. Rinse and pat dry with paper towels. Cut beans diagonally into halves or thirds, depending on size; set aside.

Trim ends from zucchini, rinse, and pat dry with paper towels. On a cutting board, slice in half lengthwise. With the flat side facing down, cut into quarters. Slice crosswise into ¼-inch widths and set aside.

Pour olive oil into a large (5-quart, or preferably a little larger) saucepan. Add onion and garlic and cook on medium heat 2-3 minutes or until soft, stirring occasionally. Add carrots, celery, parsley, 1 teaspoon salt, and dash pepper; stir until combined well. Cook 3-4 minutes, stirring occasionally.

Add chicken stock to vegetable mixture and bring to a boil. Add potatoes, green beans, zucchini, peas, tomatoes, tomato juice, 1 teaspoon salt, dash pepper, and sugar. Stir until combined well and bring to a boil. Reduce heat to medium-low and cook, uncovered, for 20-25 minutes, or until potatoes are cooked through, stirring occasionally. Adjust to taste. Serve hot.

Ham Stock

When my mother arrived home with smoked ham shanks from the local butcher, I knew she was about to prepare the stock for Old-Fashioned Split Pea Soup (opposite page).

Mysteriously, some kind of wonderful magic happens after the Ham Stock simmers for a few hours. The deep, rich character it adds to the Split Pea is unmistakable. As for the flavorful ham meat, only a small amount will be used in the soup, so consider repurposing the remainder for other occasions—in omelets, sandwiches or served alongside mashed potatoes and gravy. Mmmm, yum.

Makes about 2 quarts

3 (4-5 pounds) smoked ham shanks*

1 medium onion, peeled and quartered

2 medium unpeeled carrots, rinsed and quartered crosswise

2 medium ribs celery, rinsed and quartered crosswise

3 sprigs fresh thyme

3 sprigs flat-leaf (Italian) parsley

Water

(*Note: If possible, ask the butcher to crack the bones.)

Trim excess fat from ham shanks; discard. Rinse shanks and place inside a large (20-25 quart) stockpot, or the largest pot you have on hand. Add onion, carrots, celery, thyme, and parsley, and fill pot three-quarters full with water. Bring to a boil, then reduce to medium heat. Cook for 3 hours, partially covered, adding 2 cups water midway through.

Transfer ham shanks to a cutting board; set aside. Using a slotted spoon, remove the vegetables and ham scraps; discard. Position a fine mesh strainer or colander over a 5-quart saucepan. Pour the stock through the strainer and discard remnants. Refrigerate the stock, covered, overnight. The next day, scrape off the top layer of fat. *Or,* if making Split Pea Soup right away, pour stock in batches into a fat separator and degrease. Otherwise, use stock within 3-4 days or freeze in an airtight container.

Trim fat from cooked shanks and measure ¾ cup of finely chopped meat. Cover with plastic and store in the refrigerator for Old-Fashioned Split Pea Soup. Use leftover meat for another occasion or discard.

Old-Fashioned Split Pea Soup

My mother's favorite color was green. Besides it appearing on sweaters and blouses, she often wore a costume emerald brooch with diamonds (the same brooch that now gives me a pass on getting pinched every St. Patrick's Day). This hue also showed up around her home— on dishware, porcelain planters, or as an accent on throw rugs. Furthermore, my mother had a green thumb, and nurtured her plants with loving care.

Green reminds me of the time I hosted Irish Night for one of our Gourmet Club dinners. A lack of menu collaboration amongst our members resulted in a comical sight. Everyone brought beverages and courses that were every tint, tone, and shade of green imaginable— Midori Sours, cabbage, Grasshopper Pie, Marsh Mints, and more. Even my dress was cloverleaf, to say nothing of the table setting. Evidently, that night we gourmets goofed.

I must admit I never shared my mother's affinity for green, preferring instead other colors on the wheel, like reds, blues, and yellows. I think that's why I shied away from Split Pea Soup for so long. Could it have been its olive-drab appearance? I don't know, but my mother made it often. I think it was her favorite.

It seems that people fall into two camps: those who love Split Pea, and those who don't. If you fall into the latter category, here's some encouraging news—give my mother's recipe a try! I did and have been making it every since. Her Ham Stock gives this velvety soup rich character, and the tender bits of meat from the hocks add hearty flavor and appealing texture. Green is winking, after all.

Serves 6 to 8

1 recipe Ham Stock
   (opposite page)

¾ cup reserved chopped ham
   (from Ham Stock, opposite page)

1 (16-ounce) package green
   split peas

¼ cup extra virgin olive oil

1 medium onion, finely chopped

2 medium stalks celery,
   finely chopped

1 medium carrot, peeled and
   finely chopped

Salt and freshly ground
   black pepper

½ teaspoon fresh thyme

1 bay leaf

3 cups water, or as needed

Rinse split peas in a colander. Drain and set aside.

Pour olive oil into a large (5-quart) saucepan. Add onion, celery, carrots, ½ teaspoon salt, and dash pepper. Stir together and cook on medium heat for 5 minutes or until vegetables are soft.

Add prepared ham stock and bring to a boil. Add split peas, thyme, and bay leaf; stir to combine well. Reduce heat to medium and cook, partially covered, for about 50 minutes, stirring occasionally.

Add 3 cups water, stir, and continue to cook for another 20-25 minutes. Adjust to taste. Discard bay leaf. Add reserved chopped ham; stir. Serve hot. *(Note: To reheat soup, heat soup through completely. If needed, add ½ cup water at a time.)*

Salads

Beet Salad with Candied Walnuts and Feta   84

Herbed Black-Eyed Peas Salad with Feta   87

Butter Lettuce Salad with Lemon Mustard Dressing   89

Pam's Vinaigrette Dressing   91

Cabbage Salad with Olive Oil and Lemon Dressing   93

Chicken Salad   95

Fresh Mixed Green Salad   97

Lemon Pineapple Chiffon Mold   98

Cold Mediterranean Pasta Salad   101

Spinach and Bell Pepper Salad with Feta   103

Beet Salad with Candied Walnuts and Feta
Salata Tefla me Karydia ke Feta

Poor leafy beet stems—they usually get tossed in favor of the more prominent bulb, but these verdant greens and their stems are tasty, nutritious, and among my favorites.

A photo inspired this recipe. It incorporates the whole beet—from to top to bottom—into a delicious, interesting, and satisfying salad that can be served warm or cold. The nuts add surprise, and feta a creamy bite. Just remember, beets leave a reddish stain on your hands or clothes so you may want to wear protective gloves and an apron when handling them.

Serves 4

1 medium bunch red beets with greens attached

2 tablespoons extra virgin olive oil

2 medium cloves garlic, finely chopped

Juice from ½ lemon

Salt and freshly ground black pepper to taste

¼ cup candied walnuts or pecans, broken into small pieces

2 ounces feta cheese, crumbled

Trim ends from bulbs; discard. Trim base from stems; discard.

For the Bulbs: Scrub under cold water to remove dirt and place inside a medium saucepan. Cover with water and bring to a boil. Cook, uncovered, for 35 minutes, or until bulbs are tender and can be easily pierced with a fork. With a slotted spoon, transfer to a plate and cool 10-15 minutes. Remove skin; discard skin. Slice the cooked bulbs into bite-size chunks and place in bowl; set aside.

For the Leafy Green Stems: Rinse under cold water to remove dirt; shake off excess water. On a cutting board, gather stems like a bouquet and slice crosswise into 1-inch widths; set aside.

Pour olive oil into a large (12-inch) nonstick skillet. Add garlic and cook on medium heat until garlic starts to sizzle. Add greens and stems, cooked beets, lemon juice, and season with salt and pepper. Turn with tongs to mix and cook until greens are wilted and stems tender, about 4-5 minutes. Transfer to a serving bowl. Adjust to taste. Add candied walnuts and toss. Add crumbled feta cheese; serve.

Herbed Black-Eyed Peas Salad with Feta
Salata Mavromatika me Votanaka ke Feta

Whether peas, beans, or lentils, Greeks love legumes. They're just as popular served in soups and salads as they are in entrees. It's easy to understand why. These seeds suit the hot Mediterranean climate, especially the dry, barren conditions of the Cycladic Islands. Besides, they're economical and provide an exceptional source of protein and fiber.

Included in the ranks is the humble black-eyed pea. Here, herbs and celery embolden their smooth, creamy texture to make this cold salad a fulfilling side dish for any spring or summer meal.

Serves 4 to 6

½ pound dried black-eyed peas

Water

1 medium rib celery, finely chopped

½ cup loosely packed flat-leaf (Italian) parsley, finely chopped

2 teaspoons fresh thyme

½ teaspoon salt

Dash freshly ground black pepper

4 ounces feta cheese, crumbled

½ cup Pam's Vinaigrette Dressing (see page 91)

Advance Preparation: Place beans in a large a bowl and cover with water. Soak overnight; drain in a colander.

Fill a large (5-quart) saucepan three-quarters full with water and bring to a boil. Add drained beans and return to a boil. Reduce heat to medium and cook, uncovered, for 30 minutes, or until the peas are tender; drain in a colander.

Add celery, parsley, thyme, ½ teaspoon salt, and dash pepper; stir to combine well. Refrigerate until beans have cooled, about 1 hour, stirring occasionally to release steam.

When the mixture has cooled, add the feta cheese and dressing; stir to combine well. Adjust to taste. Refrigerate until ready to serve.

Butter Lettuce Salad
with Lemon Mustard Dressing

My mother was blessed with excellent taste in the classic European style. Take how she dressed, for instance. Wherever she went she was sure to turn a head or two. Whether it was a skirt, pumps, and cashmere cardigan draped around her shoulders, or Bermuda shorts, a linen blouse and flats, her appearance was well-considered and polished.

Her discernment also ruled her choice of accessories and furnishings for the home, such as the hammered brass bowl that sat on our baby grand piano, or the handsome walnut dining table and buffet in our dining room. Even the way she set that table for dinner guests—with white linen or lace tablecloths, cream Lenox china rimmed with gold, and flowers she effortlessly arranged for the centerpiece—delivered panache. Simplicity was her only rule.

This recipe for Butter Lettuce Salad with Lemon Mustard Dressing reminds me of my mother's timeless elegance. I came across it years ago for one of our Gourmet Club dinners, and have served it hundreds of times since.

Butter lettuce (also known as Bibb or Boston lettuce) has a soft leaf and mild flavor, so it pairs beautifully with this special sweet and pungent dressing. Consider adding other ingredients, such as mandarin oranges and toasted pine nuts in the fall or thin slices of red bell pepper during the holidays. But whatever you do, keep it simple. This salad has enough oomph to go it alone. (Original source unknown.)

Serves 4 to 6

2 large heads butter lettuce

Dressing
6 tablespoons canola oil

2 ½ tablespoons lemon juice (about 1 lemon)

3 ¼ teaspoons sugar

1 teaspoon salt

1 medium clove garlic, grated

½ teaspoon Dijon mustard

Dash freshly ground black pepper

Trim stem from lettuce heads; discard. Discard blemished leaves and the tougher dark parts from the outer leaves. Rinse, shake off excess water, and pat dry with paper towels. Tear leaves into large, bite-size pieces and place in a serving bowl. Cover with plastic and refrigerate until ready to serve.

For the Dressing: In a small bowl, place the canola oil, lemon juice, sugar, salt, garlic, mustard, and pepper; stir with a fork until combined well. Adjust to taste. Cover with plastic and refrigerate until ready to serve. Stir dressing to refresh and add to salad; toss. Serve immediately.

Pam's Vinaigrette Dressing

I don't ever recall a time when my mother purchased bottled salad dressing. Instead, she made it from scratch every night. Mostly it was vinaigrette, but on occasion she made Roquefort or Thousand Island. These dressings weren't anything complicated, nor did she follow a strict formula, but they were always fresh and homemade.

I suppose the old adage is true—the apple doesn't fall very far from the tree. After I moved into an apartment of my own, I continued in the same tradition. As a matter of fact, the shelves that stocked the bottled version in the market seemed alien. That is, until I got married and had a busy family of my own.

Then, it seemed like I was always running to the store to buy some rendition of vinaigrette. After all, it's so convenient to just untwist and pour. But aside from the expense that kept adding up, I started noticing something missing—its taste lacked the gusto I craved.

That's when I came up with this recipe. It's not only more economical (most of the ingredients can be purchased in bulk), but full of piquant flavor. Now, there's always a fresh batch waiting in the refrigerator.

If the above saying is true, then so must this: If the apple does fall far from the tree, somehow it always finds its way back home.

Makes 5 ½ cups

7 cloves garlic, peeled

1 (2-ounce) can anchovy fillets

1 ½ cups distilled white vinegar, or red or white wine vinegar

2 teaspoons salt

½ teaspoon freshly ground black pepper

2 teaspoons oregano

2 teaspoons Dijon mustard

2 tablespoons sugar

3 cups canola oil

Place the garlic in a food processor and process completely. Add the anchovies and process completely. Add vinegar, salt, pepper, oregano, Dijon mustard, and sugar and process for 30 seconds. Add the oil and process for another 30 seconds, or until the mixture is thoroughly combined. Adjust to taste. Pour into an airtight container and refrigerate. Will stay fresh for at least 1 month.

Cabbage Salad with Olive Oil and Lemon Dressing
Lahanosalata

This salad is refreshing, simple, and nutritious, and offers a welcome alternative to the usual leafy variety.

Serves 4

½ medium (2½ to 3-pound) green cabbage

¾ cup loosely packed flat-leaf (Italian) parsley, finely chopped

<u>Dressing</u>

3 tablespoons extra virgin olive oil

2 tablespoons lemon juice

½ teaspoon salt

Dash freshly ground black pepper

To clean the cabbage, remove any discolored outer leaves. Rinse and pat dry with paper towels. With a sharp knife, cut the cabbage in half through the stem. Put one of the halves back in the refrigerator for another occasion. For the remaining half, make two upside-down V slits on either side of the core and remove core; discard. Shred finely and place in a medium bowl. Add parsley and place in the refrigerator until ready to serve.

For the Dressing: Place olive oil, lemon juice, salt, and pepper in a small bowl and beat with a fork until combined well. Cover with plastic and refrigerate until ready to serve. Add dressing to salad and toss well. Adjust to taste; serve cold.

Chicken Salad

Everyone loves a good chicken salad, but the problem is finding one. So after becoming disappointed with the store and restaurant versions, I decided to get to work in my kitchen.

First, I envisioned tender, hearty bite-size chunks of meat cast in the lead role. Then, I conjured a few additional ingredients as supporting characters for texture, interest, and flavor. Only one question remained. How could I assure the chicken's succulence instead of ending up with a dry, chewy bite? The solution lay in the cooking method. Steaming the premium part of the fowl—the breast—ensures it retains plenty of moisture. This recipe probably won't win an Academy Award, but it does finally satisfy my longing for a simple, luscious chicken salad.

Serves 4 to 6

2 pounds boneless, skinless chicken breasts

Water

2 medium ribs celery, finely chopped

½ cup loosely packed flat-leaf (Italian) parsley, finely chopped

½ cup regular or low-fat mayonnaise

1 teaspoon salt

Dash freshly ground black pepper

Insert a steam basket inside a large (5-quart) saucepan. Fill pot with just enough water to reach the bottom of the basket. Rinse breasts and place inside basket. Bring to a boil and cook, covered, about 8-10 minutes. Turn breasts over and cook for another 8-10 minutes, adding water to the pot as needed, or until a knife inserted in the thickest part of the meat is white, not pink. Transfer the meat to a cutting board; cool about 10 minutes.

With a sharp knife, cut chicken into bite-size chunks and place in a bowl.

Add celery, parsley, mayonnaise, salt, and pepper, and stir until combined well. Adjust to taste. Cover with plastic and refrigerate until ready to serve. Add on top of Fresh Mixed Green Salad (see page 97), or use as a sandwich filling.

Fresh Mixed Green Salad

Little else offers the versatility of a classic mixed green salad—it goes with just about everything. But there are a couple important things to consider when using lettuce heads versus the prepackaged variety. One is making sure the leaves are cleaned ahead of time—either early that morning or the day before—so they have a chance to become cold and crisp, the secret to a successful salad. (To do this, trim the stems and discard the tough outer and blemished leaves. Then rinse and shake off excess water before placing the cleaned leaves in a plastic bag and inside the refrigerator.)

The second is water control. Who enjoys eating soggy, drippy leaves? To avoid this common problem, be sure to remove excess moisture with paper towels or a salad spinner before tearing the leaves and placing them inside the bowl. Besides, a dry leaf ensures the dressing adheres well.

With these bumps out of the way, your salad is sure to be a winner. Then, when all the ingredients are finally assembled, take a moment to revel in green's many guises—fern, meadow, forest, celery, and granny smith apple.

Serves 6

10 leaves Romaine lettuce*

10 leaves red leaf lettuce*

4 fresh green onions (scallions), thinly sliced

3 medium ribs celery, finely chopped

1 medium green bell pepper, julienned

1 medium cucumber, peeled and thinly sliced

½ cup loosely packed flat-leaf (Italian) parsley, finely chopped

½ cup Pam's Vinaigrette Dressing (see page 91)

(*Note: Consider also adding a wedge of iceberg lettuce for extra texture.)

Advance Preparation: Prepare lettuce as described above.

Tear leaves into large bite-size pieces and place in a large serving bowl. Add fresh green onions, celery, bell peppers, cucumbers, and parsley. Cover with plastic and refrigerate until ready to serve. Add dressing and toss well to coat; serve.

Lemon and Pineapple Chiffon Mold

Gelatin molds aren't as popular as they once were, but curiously, many buffets include at least one. I think I know why. These cold, wiggly salads are refreshing counterparts to the staid and usual. This delicious lemon recipe has been in our family for years, and it never fails to receive rave reviews. Crushed pineapple adds texture to the mold's otherwise light, fluffy character.

Serves 14

Vegetable oil for greasing mold

2 (3.4-ounce) packages lemon gelatin

Water

2 cups miniature marshmallows

1 (8-ounce) package cream cheese

½ pint heavy whipping cream

1 (8-ounce) can crushed pineapple, drained

Red seedless grapes for garnish (optional)

Grease a 9-quart mold with a little vegetable oil; set aside.

Pour 2 cups water in a medium (3-quart) saucepan and bring to a boil. Remove pot from burner and add gelatin; stir until dissolved. Pour into a large bowl and add 1 cup cold water and marshmallows; stir. Refrigerate for 1½ hours, or until the mixture has gelled but is still loose and not completely set, stirring every 30 minutes. Remove from refrigerator and set aside.

Soften cream cheese in the microwave for 20-30 seconds and place in a medium bowl. Sir with a wooden spoon until it resembles the consistency of thick yogurt.

In a separate bowl, beat the heavy whipping cream with a portable electric mixer until stiff. Add whipped cream to the cream cheese and blend together on low speed until combined well.

Add drained pineapple to cream cheese mixture and blend on low speed until combined well.

Add cream cheese mixture to gelatin mixture and blend on low speed until combined well. Pour into prepared mold and refrigerate overnight.

Before ready to serve, unmold and place on a serving platter. Garnish the center with red seedless grapes, if desired.

Cold Mediterranean Pasta Salad

Here's a robust-flavored salad I concocted with some of my favorite ingredients. I especially love those sumptuous mouthfuls where bits of cheese, artichoke, and herbs get lodged inside the pasta shell. The dressing adds yet another layer of delicious flavor. The key to this recipe's success is allotting the ingredients in equal proportions so no single one dominates.

Serves 4 to 6

½ **pound shell pasta**

1 ½ **tablespoons extra virgin olive oil**

¾ **teaspoon salt**

¾ **cup marinated artichokes, drained and coarsely chopped**

½ **cup pitted Kalamata olives, drained**

⅓ **cup julienne-sliced sun-dried tomatoes in olive oil, drained**

¼ **cup loosely packed flat-leaf (Italian) parsley**

1 **teaspoon finely chopped fresh tarragon**

4 **ounces feta cheese, crumbled**

½ **cup Pam's Vinaigrette Dressing (see page 91), plus extra on hand**

Cook pasta al dente according to package directions; drain in a colander. Place cooked pasta in large serving bowl and add olive oil and salt; stir to combine. Refrigerate for 1 hour to cool.

After the pasta has cooled for one hour, add the artichokes, olives, sun-dried tomatoes, parsley, tarragon, and cheese. Toss until blended well; refrigerate. When ready to serve, add dressing and toss again. Adjust to taste; serve cold.

Spinach and Bell Pepper Salad with Feta
Spanaki kai Piperi Salata me Feta

Summer is about spending time in the open air. So, when one of our Gourmet Club members noticed an ad in the paper saying a Picnic Basket Contest was going to be held at Golden Gate Park in San Francisco during a series of musical performances, we took our feast to the great outdoors. It would be our final gala after three memorable years.

On the day of the contest, we lugged armloads from our kitchens: Homemade Pickles and Preserves, a Timbale Pasta Salad, and a Turkey Roll Stuffed with Spinach and Prosciutto. To add to our ingenious menu, we brought homemade bread shaped into a treble clef and sugar cookies fashioned into musical notes to jibe with the musical theme of the afternoon. We were certain these novelties would satisfy the competition's criteria for originality, and had no doubt our delicious spread and hard work would garner a ribbon amongst the hundreds of other entries. Quietly, we started planning our victory celebration.

When the judges showed up at our station with their clipboards, we beamed proudly. Later on when the authorities announced the winners, we listened attentively for our name to be called.

Would you believe our picnic basket didn't even place? Apparently, our egos bit off more than we could chew. Forlorn only momentarily, our dashed spirits got quickly replaced with gratitude and joy for the good times had over the past three years. The Gourmet Club was now officially adjourned.

Of course, you don't need to enter a picnic basket competition when summertime arrives in your backyard. When scheming your next warm-weather menu, consider this Spinach and Bell Pepper Salad with Feta. I stumbled upon the original version while perusing a home-style magazine, and I was inspired to make it my own. I love its attractive and colorful display of vegetables. Who knows? It just might provoke you, too, to be invigorated by the possibilities of the season.

Serves 8

1 medium bunch fresh spinach

2 large red bell peppers (¾-1 pound)

2 large yellow bell peppers (¾-1 pound)

5 fresh green onions (scallions), finely sliced

1 cup loosely packed flat-leaf (Italian) parsley, finely chopped

3-4 ounces feta cheese, crumbled

About ½ cup of Pam's Vinaigrette Dressing (see page 91)

Trim stems from spinach; discard.

To clean the spinach leaves, soak in a container of cold water so dirt particles fall to the bottom. Remove leaves and discard dirty water. Repeat once more. Drain leaves and pat dry with paper towels.

Tear leaves into large bite-size pieces and arrange on a large oval platter, slightly overlapping the edges.

Core yellow bell peppers and slice crosswise into ½-inch-thick rings. Trim the pith and seeds; discard. Rinse and pat dry with paper towels. Arrange in a single row over the spinach, slightly overlapping the edges.

Repeat for the red bell peppers, placing a second row alongside the yellow one.

Add the sliced green onions over the bell peppers, distributing evenly. Repeat for the chopped parsley, then the crumbled feta. Cover with plastic and refrigerate until ready to serve.

Drizzle about ½ cup of Pam's Vinaigrette Dressing over the salad and serve with tongs.

Bready Things

Cinnamon Coffee Cake

Waking up to warm, homemade cinnamon coffee cake is one of life's simple pleasures. This recipe's a favorite in our home, especially on Christmas morning. Besides, the aroma is delightful—at least, that's what they tell me. (Adapted: Source Unknown.)

Makes 15 pieces

Sugar and Cinnamon Mixture

1½ cups firmly packed light brown sugar

3 tablespoons all-purpose flour, plus a little extra for the baking pan

3 tablespoons ground cinnamon

1 cup (two sticks) butter, melted

Batter

3 cups all-purpose flour

1 tablespoon baking powder

1 teaspoon salt

1 cup (2 sticks) butter, softened

1½ cups sugar

3 eggs

1 cup milk

1 teaspoon vanilla extract

For the Sugar-Cinnamon Mixture: Grease and flour a 13 x 9 x 2-inch baking pan; set aside. Place brown sugar, 3 tablespoons flour, and cinnamon in a medium bowl. Stir with a fork until combined well, breaking up clumps with your fingers; set aside.

Melt 1 cup butter; set aside.

For the Batter: Preheat oven to 350 degrees. Place flour, baking powder, and salt in a medium bowl; set aside.

Place 1 cup softened butter in a large mixing bowl and beat for 1 minute. Gradually add sugar and beat until fluffy, stopping once to scrape down the sides of the bowl.

Add the eggs one at a time, stopping once or twice to scrape.

Measure milk. Add vanilla to milk and stir with a fork until combined well. Set aside.

Add one-third of the flour mixture to the butter mixture and blend on low speed just until the flour dissolves into the batter. Add one-third of the milk mixture and blend; stop to scrape. Repeat 2 more times.

Pour half of the batter into the prepared pan, and spread evenly with a spatula. Add half of the cinnamon mixture, and then half of the melted butter, distributing evenly.

Add the remaining batter by dropping spoonfuls with a large metal spoon. With a rubber spatula, gently push the batter so it covers evenly. Add the remaining cinnamon mixture, and then the remaining butter, distributing evenly.

Place in preheated oven. Cook for 35 minutes, or until the cake has slightly pulled away from the edges of the pan and a knife inserted in the center comes out clean. Cool for 20 minutes. Using a sharp knife, cut into pieces and transfer to a serving platter. Serve warm.

Hotcakes

How I couldn't wait to eat my mother's hotcakes on weekend mornings! Covered with melted butter and syrup, they always made my tummy smile. Unlike the thick, fluffy ones found in the coffee shop, these are thin and light with a silky texture. As tradition goes, even our adult children still welcome a plate of their own.

4 to 6 Servings

2 cups pancake baking mix

2 eggs

1¼ cups plus 1 tablespoon low-fat milk

Nonstick cooking spray

Butter

Maple syrup

Place baking mix in a medium bowl. Add eggs and milk. Stir vigorously with a whisk until smooth; set aside.

Apply nonstick spray to a large (12- to 13-inch) nonstick skillet; wipe lightly with a paper napkin to remove excess oil.

Heat on medium-high until very hot. Reduce heat to medium and pour ¼ cup of batter into the pan. Repeat 2 more times (or as space in the pan allows). Cook until surface forms bubbles. Flip hotcakes over with a spatula and place 1 teaspoon butter over each one. Cook about 15 seconds, or until underside is golden brown; transfer to a plate. Repeat until all the batter is gone, making sure to whisk occasionally so the mixture gets recombined.

Drizzle maple syrup over each serving; serve hot.

The Best Sourdough Croutons

I must admit I'm a hopeless bread aficionado. But I know I'm not alone. Many of you, too, would choose a fresh, soft and crusty chew over the sugary experience esteemed by our sweet comrades. So you can understand my plight when attempting to find hearty, tasty croutons at the grocery store for our nightly salads. Not that there's anything wrong with the store-bought kind, but let's just say those cookie-cutter morsels still left me hankering for my daily provision of bread.

One day, I was encouraged when I visited a specialty cheese shop and happened upon an enticing cellophane bag of "gourmet" croutons. With high hopes, I brought it home only to be disheartened once again. They were stale. This time I resolved to make my own.

By now, I've made these chunky, flavorful croutons hundreds of times, and always begin with the freshest and most delicious sourdough bread available. Plus, they're as equally fit as noshes as they are in soups or salads. Now, only one problem remains—always having to refill the stockpile. These get devoured quickly.

Makes 1 batch

1 large (1-1 ½ pounds) loaf fresh sourdough bread

½-¾ cup extra virgin olive oil (depending on size of loaf)

3-5 tablespoons grated Parmesan cheese (depending on size of loaf)

Salt and freshly ground black pepper

Preheat the oven to 350 degrees.

Slice bread into 1-inch-thick slices. Cut each slice into halves, then quarters, then eighths (depending on loaf size) and place in an extra-large bowl. Add one-third of the olive oil over the bread. Add one-third of the cheese and season generously with salt and pepper. Toss well to coat. Repeat 2 more times.

Pour onto 2 large (15 x 10 x 1-inch) ungreased baking sheets. Slide baking sheets back and forth on a flat surface until croutons fall into a single layer. Place in preheated oven and cook for 15-17 minutes, or until golden; cool. Store in an airtight container. Will stay fresh for up to 3 weeks.

Challah Bread Stuffing

As my mother filled my porcelain cup with hot tea from the kettle, I thought about how fortunate I was that she lived only a mile away; my frequent visits brought us both comfort. We never seemed to be at a loss for words when we sat around her kitchen table. My mother loved hearing stories about her grandchildren—*"haramou"* ("my joy") she called them—or about what was going on that day. As for me, I savored her snippets of wisdom that seemed ideally suited to the moment. "In Greek we have a saying…" she would say before translating the expression into English.

On this particular day, the conversation drifted to her childhood. She smiled as she spoke about those unbridled summers on the beach in Greece, or the evenings singing in harmony with her brothers and sisters. But soon her grin vanished, and a somber look washed over her face.

"What is it, Mom?" I asked

She paused lost in thought while staring off into the distance. Then she looked at me and said, "I have known hunger." At once I knew what would be coming next, and braced myself. I knew she wasn't referring to those familiar stomach growls from eating a couple hours later than usual, or missing a meal altogether. She meant the kind of hunger that eats away at your soul; that shames and says you're unworthy.

She continued, "In 1937, the leader of the Greek Orthodox Archdiocese in America, Archbishop Athenagoras, was getting concerned about the growing number of Greek immigrants arriving here. The situation created a shortage of churches, priests, and schools, not to mention worries over how the Greek language and culture would be preserved. My father and other Orthodox priests like him were appointed to go to America and help. So my father left Greece with the intention of returning in a year or two. But it didn't go as he planned. His work called him to serve parishes in Mason City, Iowa; Canton, Ohio; Milwaukee, Wisconsin; and several towns in New Jersey before finally settling at Holy Trinity Church in San Francisco. Meanwhile, war broke out in Europe."

"And you and your family had to endure the war without your father," I said.

"Yes," she replied. "It wasn't so hard with the Italians. But we really suffered with the Germans."

"Tell me again, Mom," I said while leaning closer.

"In 1941, Germany bombed our ports in Salonika and Patras. Then, the German soldiers marched into Athens where I lived. I was fourteen years old," she replied.

"Oh, Mom, how terrifying that must have been," I said.

"When the Germans arrived in Athens, they were malnourished, without food and supplies. Soon after, they started stealing from the people. They stripped our factories, plants, homes, and offices. Above all, they took our food. The Germans stole from our markets and restaurants, and seized produce from our farms. Within a short time, they occupied all of

Greece. It wasn't long until even our food distribution system stopped altogether. Athens and Piraeus were the hardest hit," my mother said.

"How did you eat?" I asked.

"With my father gone, my mother, who had retired from teaching, was home alone caring for me and my siblings. She had no food to give us. Besides, you could only buy the basics, like bread and potatoes, through the high-priced Black Market system. My mother had very little money. Fortunately, my *Thio* (Uncle) Thanassis owned a leather business and was well off. He helped us so we could eat," she said.

"Despite the Occupation, we had to go on with our lives. My brother Tony and I walked to school every day, and we saw people collapsing in the streets from hunger. Then the trucks would come and take away the bodies. Sometimes we even had to stretch our legs over them just so we could pass by," she recounted while getting up from her chair to simulate the act. "We got very thin, especially my brother," she added.

My mother continued, "We ended up being separated from my father for ten years. During much of that time, he didn't know if we were dead or alive because all communication had been shut down. Finally, a few years after the war, we reunited with him in San Francisco. My father had bought a home there. But then *Thio* Thanassis came for a visit. He asked my father to repay him for the money he spent on food to keep us alive. So my father sold our home to compensate him," she concluded while I took the last sip from my porcelain teacup and looked into her sensitive green eyes.

Driving home that afternoon, images of my mother's story during the Great Famine of World War II swirled in my head. Undoubtedly, her experience helped shape her resilient character that served her well throughout her life. It also forged her grateful attitude for the simple pleasures in life, such as a glass of wine, a slice of freshly baked bread with butter, a visit with a close friend or relative, or a beautiful, sunny day—all of which made her smile. Then it came to me. Those wise sayings she told me again and again—"Always stand strong and dignified, like the Acropolis, and don't ever let anything or anyone take you down," and her oft-used phrase, "Never throw good food away."

*

So when gathering around the table, let us consider our many blessings, especially Thanksgiving Day.

My parents created this Challah Bread Stuffing recipe many years ago, and I can still imagine them hovering side by side over the stove discussing each addition. Since then, not a holiday has passed without this fluffy, soufflé-like dish at our table.

Here are a few tips. First, to save time and energy, consider toasting the bread the day before and storing it in an airtight bag. Second, I encourage you to prepare the remaining ingredients and organize them near the stove before starting so you can add them as the recipe calls—that is, if you want to remain calm during the process. And, finally, don't forget to stuff the turkey! The drippings from the bones and tendons add yet another layer of delicious flavor. Besides, it's fun to do and a sight to behold. Then, take a moment to bow your head in gratitude for the abundance before you—Amen.

Serves 8

Bread

A 1-pound fresh loaf Challah bread (preferably with sesame seeds, if available), sliced

Remainder

6 tablespoons (⅓ cup) butter

1 medium onion

4 fresh green onions (scallions), finely sliced

4 medium ribs celery, finely chopped

¾ cup loosely packed flat-leaf (Italian) parsley, finely chopped

½ cup dry white wine, such as Chardonnay

3 chicken bouillon cubes, roughly chopped

1 teaspoon salt

Dash freshly ground black pepper

2 (14-ounce) cans chicken broth

½ cup water

1 cup grated Monterey Jack cheese

½ cup grated Parmesan cheese

6 eggs, lightly beaten

For the Bread: Preheat oven to 325 degrees. Arrange bread slices in a single layer on a large (15 x 10 x 1-inch) baking sheet. Place in preheated oven and cook for 10-12 minutes, or until underside is light golden. Turn over and cook another 4-5 minutes. Cool about 5 minutes. Tear toasted bread into large bite-size pieces and continue with recipe, or store in a plastic bag until ready to proceed.

For the Remainder: Melt butter in a large (5-quart) saucepan. Add the onion and cook on medium heat until soft, about 2-3 minutes, stirring occasionally. Add green onions, celery, parsley, wine, water, bouillon cubes, salt, and dash pepper; stir until combined well. Cook for 5 minutes, uncovered, until vegetables are soft and bouillon cubes dissolved; stir occasionally.

Add toasted bread pieces and chicken broth. Turn the mixture with a wooden spoon until all of the bread is moist.

Add the Monterey Jack and Parmesan cheeses and stir until melted.

Add the lightly beaten eggs; stir to combine well. Cook for 10-15 minutes on medium heat, or until the eggs have set, stirring continually so the mixture doesn't stick too much to the bottom of the pot. *(Note: Some sticking is to be expected.)* Adjust to taste. Transfer to a large bowl and cool. Cover bowl with plastic and refrigerate until ready to stuff the turkey.

To prepare the turkey cavity for stuffing, rinse the interior of the cavity and pat dry; season generously with salt and pepper. Spoon the stuffing inside until packed full. When ready to carve the turkey, spoon the stuffing into a serving bowl; serve hot.

Simple Once~Baked Toasts
Paximadia

For Greeks, dry, hard toasts have long been a breakfast staple. As a matter of fact, when I was growing up our kitchen drawer was never without a supply, especially when my y*iayia* (grandmother) came to visit. These toasts *(paximadia)* are usually paired with salty kasseri cheese or ham, but I prefer mine spread with butter and immersed in my morning coffee. Dunkers anyone?

Paximadia can also be enjoyed as a healthy afternoon snack: First, swipe a slice several times under running water for it to soften (hence, giving it the nickname "wet bread"). Then, drizzle on some olive oil and a tad of vinegar, and add oregano, salt, and pepper, and you're set!

So simple—yet satisfying—is the bread of life.

12 pieces

1 pound loaf country bread, preferably sourdough

Preheat oven to 350 degrees.

Slice bread crosswise into 1-inch thickness and arrange on a baking sheet. Place in preheated oven and cook for 25-30 minutes, or until the side facing down is golden. Turn slices over, being careful not to burn yourself, and cook for another 10 minutes, or until that side is also golden. *(Note: cooking times will vary according to the crumb's density.)* Set aside to cool. Place slices in an airtight container and store in a cool, dry place.

Sweet Anise and Almond Biscuits
Paximadia me Glikaniso ke Trigona

My mother loved these sweet hard biscuits, and shared them often with family, friends, and co-workers. They're similar to the Italian biscotti, and are delectable with a hot cup of tea or coffee. Plus, because they're twice baked, they stay fresh for at least several weeks.

With anise's (also called aniseed) two-dimensional flavor—first sweet, then black licorice—people seem to either love it or not. Just like anything else, don't let one or two ingredients spoil the fun when you find a recipe that grabs your attention. Simply do the next best thing. Either omit or substitute it with another one of your favorite fixings.

Makes 7 dozen

Biscuits

1 ½ cups raw almonds with skin

4 ½ cups all-purpose flour, plus a little extra

2 ¼ teaspoons baking powder

½ teaspoon salt

1 ½ teaspoons cinnamon

½ teaspoon cloves

2 teaspoons aniseed (optional), ground in a coffee grinder

2 ½ cups sugar

1 teaspoon lemon zest

½ teaspoon vanilla powder, or 1 teaspoon vanilla extract

½ cup buttermilk

½ teaspoon baking soda

2 eggs

½ pound (2 sticks) unsalted butter, softened

Sesame seeds (for topping)

Parchment paper

Egg Wash

1 egg yolk

2 teaspoons milk

1 teaspoon water

For the Biscuits: First, toast the almonds. Preheat oven to 325 degrees. Spread almonds evenly on a baking sheet and place in preheated oven. Cook for 12 minutes; cool about 20 minutes. Chop coarsely; set aside.

Sift together 4 ½ cups flour, baking powder, salt, cinnamon, and cloves in a large bowl; set aside.

Set aside the sugar, ground aniseed, lemon zest, and vanilla.

Measure the buttermilk. Add baking soda to the buttermilk and stir until smooth; set aside.

Separate the eggs, placing the whites and yolks in separate bowls. Beat the whites until stiff; set aside. Reserve the yolks for the next step.

Adjust 2 oven racks to the middle positions. Preheat oven to 350 degrees. Line 2 large (15 x 10 x 1-inch) baking sheets with parchment paper; set aside.

Beat the softened butter for 2 minutes. Gradually add sugar and beat until fluffy, stopping once to scrape down the sides of the bowl. Add reserved egg yolks and beat until combined well. Mix in the egg whites. Add the ground aniseed, lemon zest, and vanilla and mix until combined. Add buttermilk mixture and mix until combined well. Gradually add the flour mixture until blended, stopping once or twice to scrape. Add the nuts and blend; set aside.

For the Egg Wash: Place egg yolk in a small bowl. Add milk and water. Stir with a fork until combined well; set aside.

Divide the dough into 6 equal parts. Lightly sprinkle some flour on a wooden board and on your hands. Take 1 part of the dough and roll until it reaches 11 inches long and 2 inches wide. Transfer the roll to the prepared pan; flatten the top a little with your hand and mold the sides to form a loaf shape.

Brush the top and sides of the loaf with the prepared egg wash and sprinkle with sesame seeds. Repeat for the other 5 parts, placing 3 loaves on one pan and 3 on the other, allowing sufficient space between each loaf to spread during baking. Place pans in preheated oven and bake for about 20 minutes, or until light golden. Let cool for 15 minutes. Reduce temperature to 325 degrees.

Transfer one cooled loaf onto a cutting board. Using a serrated knife, cut loaf crosswise into $\frac{1}{2}$-inch-wide pieces and place them back on the pan, cut side down. Repeat for the remaining loaves. Place pans back in oven and bake another 6-8 minutes. Turn each piece over, being careful not to burn yourself, and cook for another 5 minutes; cool. Place in an airtight container. Will stay fresh for at least 3 weeks.

Easter Bread
Tsoureki

I've often wondered what it was like for my mother to have a Greek Orthodox priest as a dad. He was her father, yet he was everyone else's Father, too. Did she have to attend church every Sunday? Did her father recite scripture often in their home? My guess is that my *papou* (grandfather)—a dedicated priest with a likeable, easygoing personality, warm smile, and twinkling blue eyes—was not a strict dad.

As for my mother, her faith was deep and quiet with a particular devotion to the *Panagia* (Virgin Mary, Mother of Jesus). And fortunately for me, she had a relaxed attitude about regular church attendance.

On those Sundays my family did attend, the mood in the car was reserved. This, no doubt, was an omen for what would follow. All dressed up in my petticoat dress, bobby socks, black patent Mary Jane shoes, and short cotton gloves, I entered the narthex where I reverently lit a candle and kissed the icons of Jesus and Mary. Then I took my seat in the wooden pew—and there my misery began. For the next 2 hours, I sat wondering what in the world I was listening to. In those days, the service was conducted mostly in ancient Greek. On the other hand, my Greek consisted of broken, conversational phrases—*Ti kanis? Ti onoma sou? Efharisto* (How are you? What's your name? Thank you). If that wasn't enough, I had to also hear my mother's whispered reminders about proper church conduct. "Don't cross your arms or legs in church." "Don't point in church." "Use these three fingers to make your cross." I had only to look up at the domed ceiling bearing the face of Jesus to confirm my every move was being judged.

One particular Sunday, then, imagine my surprise when, after taking my seat, I looked up and saw my *papou* standing on the altar performing the liturgy. "There's *papou!* He's filling in for our priest today," my mother said as I sheepishly sank deeper into the pew.

As for Sunday school, the one time I attended was a dismal failure. I cried and hollered that under no circumstances would I return to a class full of strangers to color Jesus pictures. Fortunately, my mother agreed.

To be honest, the only part of church I enjoyed was the end. After an entire morning of fasting, the tiny piece of *antidoron* (Holy Eucharist bread) soaked in red wine awakened both my palate and me. And upon leaving, the *antidoron*'s dense crumb soothed my hungry stomach.

But above all, my favorite church food was *kolyva* (a cakelike mixture of boiled wheat berries, raisins, spices, and pomegranates covered with a thick layer of powdered sugar, provided by a family to mark the anniversary of the death of their loved one). It made my day when, standing on my tippy toes, I caught a glimpse of that snowy confection on the altar. And you can bet I grabbed a cup or two of it on my way out of church. All in all, I considered these bits of nourishment my reward for a difficult morning. On the drive home, I sighed relief—I had survived another Sunday.

In those days, God was somewhere in the distance—over by the candles and icons, around the church building, and beside the priest on Easter and Christmas. Many years would pass before I knew He wasn't that far, after all, and that Jesus didn't come to judge the world, but to save it.

*

While my *papou* spent his long career blessing the Holy Eucharist bread, my mother learned how to make it. Not the altar kind, but another reverent one—*tsoureki*, traditional sweet double-rise bread made at Easter time. Her recipe is simply yummy.

Traditionally, the dough is divided into 3 ropes and braided before getting decorated with red eggs (to symbolize the blood of Christ). But I like to keep it simple and make loaves instead. (I see legions of *yiayias* [grandmothers] and even the Holy Synod shaking their heads in disapproval.)

Many Greek churches and families also use this recipe in loaf form for the *Vasilopita* (New Year's bread) to celebrate the feast day in honor of *Agios Vasileios* (Saint Basil). For this occasion, the custom is to hide a coin somewhere inside the loaf. Whoever receives the slice with the coin is blessed with good fortune for the year, but one must certainly wait his or her turn. As tradition dictates, the first piece goes to St. Basil, the second to Christ, the third to the oldest member of the family, and so forth.

When making this bread, plan on being home about 6 hours. The good news is that for most of this time you could be working on the computer, eating lunch, doing the laundry, and taking the dog for a walk. Why? Because waiting for the dough to rise constitutes more than half this time.

Don't worry if you've never worked with yeast before—these instructions are foolproof. Just make sure to check the date on the package to make sure it's fresh. Also, before you start, decide on a warm, draft-free location for your dough to rise, such as a cold oven with a bowl of hot water positioned on the lowest shelf, or on top of the dryer while running a couple loads of laundry.

And finally, *tsoureki* calls for using ground mastic (from the mastic plant). Its flavor is similar to black licorice and can be purchased online or at Greek specialty food stores. Here, I've listed it as optional.

I remember the first time I watched my mother make this bread while writing detailed notes of each step on a yellow pad— "Keep kitchen temperature warm. No draft!" and "… while milk is getting warm, crack 4 eggs in a separate bowl" were among her directives. And I can envision her now, earnestly kneading the dough, stretching it out with the palms of her hands, gathering it together, and adding a little more flour until just right— to say nothing of my own anticipation about eating a warm slice, or even toasting a piece for breakfast and watching the butter melt into its nooks and crannies. Oh, such divine pleasure!

Makes 2 to 3 loaves

<u>**Yeast Mixture**</u>

3 (¼-ounce) packages active
  dry yeast

1½ cups warm water (100-110
  degrees using a candy
  thermometer, or 50-60 seconds
  in the microwave)

3 tablespoons sugar

<u>**Dough**</u>

1½ tablespoons melted butter,
  plus extra for greasing pans

8 cups all-purpose flour, sifted

1 teaspoon salt

1-2 teaspoons mastic (optional)

2 cups regular or low-fat (2%) milk

½ cup (1 stick) butter,
  cut up in pieces

4 eggs

¾ cup sugar

1 cup all-purpose flour
  for kneading by hand,
  plus a little extra if needed

½ teaspoon salt

<u>**Egg Wash**</u>

1 egg yolk

2 teaspoons milk

1 teaspoon water

Sesame seeds (optional)

For the Yeast Mixture: Add sugar to warm water and stir until dissolved. Add yeast; stir. Wait about 10 minutes for bubbles and foam to appear on the surface. Set aside.

For the Dough: Grease an extra-large bowl with 1½ tablespoons melted butter; set aside. Grease 3 standard size (9 x 5 x 3-inch) nonstick metal loaf pans with butter, *or* 1 standard loaf pan and 1 round (10 x 2-inch) nonstick metal cake pan; set aside.

Sift together 8 cups flour, 1 teaspoon salt, and mastic in a large bowl; set aside.

Pour milk into a saucepan and add ½ cup butter cut up into pieces. Cook on medium heat until the milk is hot, but does not boil, and butter is melted. Pour milk mixture in the large bowl of a freestanding electric mixer fitted with the standard paddle attachment.

Add yeast mixture to milk mixture and blend on low speed until combined.

In a separate bowl, beat eggs with a portable electric mixer, about 2 minutes. Gradually add sugar until combined well.

Add egg mixture to milk mixture and blend on low speed until uniform. Gradually add sifted flour mixture until combined well, stopping a couple times to scrape down the sides of the bowl with a spatula.

Replace the paddle attachment with the dough hook attachment and knead the dough on #2 speed for 5 minutes. *(Note: The dough will be soft and very gummy.)* Pour dough into the prepared extra-large bowl, using a rubber spatula to release the dough from the dough hook. Place in a warm, draft-free spot and cover with a damp, light-weight cloth, such a flour-sack towel. Let stand for 2½ hours for dough to rise.

Meanwhile, prepare for the second kneading (this time by hand). Measure 1 cup flour. Add ½ teaspoon salt and stir together with a fork. Pour half the flour mixture onto a wooden surface and spread with your hands.

After the dough has stood for 2½ hours, punch it with your fist to release air and turn onto the floured surface. Knead by hand for about 5 minutes, working in the flour on the board and adding the remaining flour a little at a time as needed. *(Note: You want the consistency to feel comfortable to handle while remaining soft and gummy.)*

If using 3 rectangular loaf pans, cut dough into thirds with a sharp knife and place in pans. Mold dough into an oval shape with your hands, being sure to leave some space around the dough. *Or,* if using one rectangular and one round pan, place one-third of the dough in the loaf pan and the remainder in the round pan. For the round pan, shape the dough into a mound, also leaving some space around the mound. Set pans aside.

For the Egg Wash: Place egg yolk, milk, and water in a small bowl and stir with a fork until combined well. Dip the ends of a pastry brush into the egg wash and wipe tops and sides of dough. Sprinkle with sesame seeds and return to a warm place to stand for 1 hour.

Place oven rack to lowest position and preheat to 350 degrees.

After the dough has stood for 1 hour, place pans in preheated oven and bake for 20 minutes. Reduce heat to 275 degrees and bake for another 30 minutes, or until golden brown. *(Note: If bread starts getting dark, cover with aluminum foil. Also, don't worry if cracks appear on the sides of the loaves while rising. That's the charm of homemade!)* Cool for 10 minutes.

Cut around the edges with a sharp knife and release the bread using oven mitts so you don't burn yourself; place on a cooling rack. Enjoy bread warm, at room temperature, or toasted. Otherwise, wrap loaves in aluminum foil and place in refrigerator.

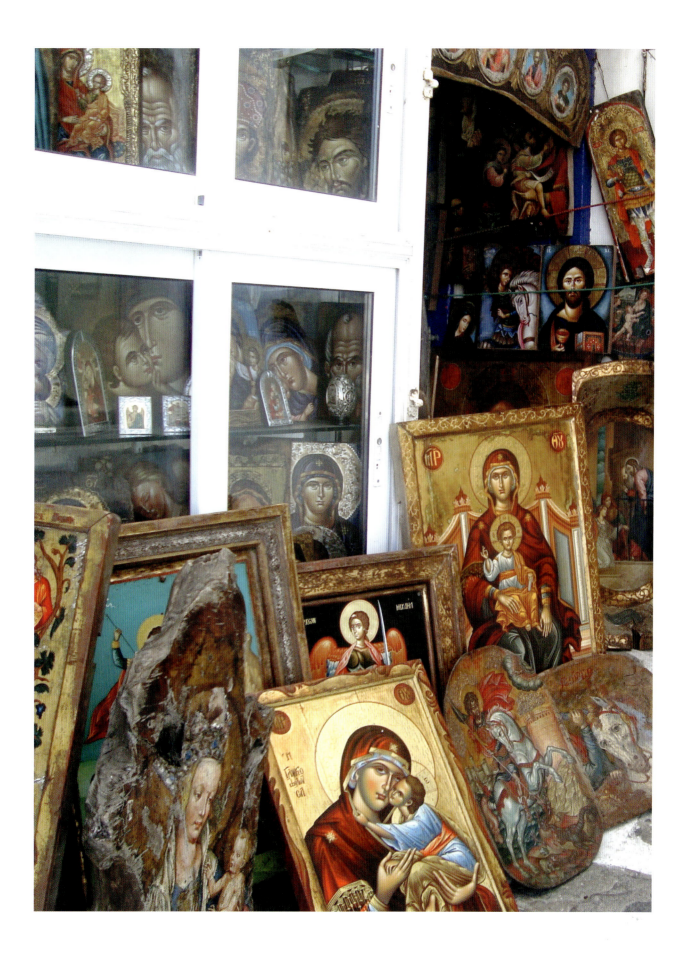

Cornbread

I'm convinced no other recipe has as many variations for suiting personal preference as cornbread. Among the legions, however, this is my favorite. It harks back to my Gourmet Club days, but has undergone a significant metamorphosis from the original.

The bread started out as a Southern one—with white corn meal, a scant sweetness, and a loose crumb. But after enduring much trial, error, and research, it crossed over into Northern territory—with yellow corn meal, extra sweetness, and a crumb that held in place. So whether Yankee or Confederate, c'mon y'all—here's an American classic you're sure to enjoy.

Makes 16 pieces

1½ cups yellow cornmeal

1½ cups all-purpose flour

2½ teaspoons baking powder

½ teaspoons baking soda

½ cup sugar

1 teaspoon salt

2 eggs, lightly beaten

4 ounces sour cream

1 cup milk

¼ cup (half a stick) butter, melted, plus a little extra for greasing pan

Position rack to the center of the oven and preheat to 400 degrees.

Grease a 9 x 9-inch metal baking pan with butter; set aside.

Place cornmeal, flour, baking powder, baking soda, sugar, and salt in a medium bowl and stir together with a fork or whisk until combined well. Make a well by pushing the mixture up the sides of the bowl.

Place the lightly beaten eggs in the bottom of the well and, using a wooden spoon, lightly stir together until the mixture is lumpy. Add sour cream. Gradually add milk, stirring after each addition until the mixture is uniform.

Add melted butter and stir until combined well.

Pour into the prepared pan and place in preheated oven. Bake for 15 minutes, or until light golden, the edges start coming away from the pan, and a knife inserted in the center comes out clean. *(Note: If dark blisters start to appear, reduce heat to 375 degrees.)* Cool for 15-20 minutes. Cut around the perimeter, then into squares. Serve.

Fritter Balls
with Honey Syrup and Cinnamon
Loukoumades

Every Labor Day weekend, Greeks and non-Greeks alike flock to our church's festival. There, scores of booths sell everything from gyros to fisherman hats while bouzouki music plays in the background. Invariably, the booth with the longest line (out the door and down the stairs) leads to *loukoumades*. These ball-shaped fritter darlings are drizzled with honey, sprinkled with walnuts and cinnamon, and have been known to transform glum to gladness after the first bite. Children love them. Teens love them. Adults love them.

Fortunately, in our home we don't need to wait for an annual festival to enjoy *loukoumades*, as evidenced by our daughter's reaction upon laying her eyes on them when she walks into the kitchen—"Mom, you made *loukoumades*!" Then she proceeds to trade fork for fingers while savoring its light, fluffy interior and sweet, crisp exterior before licking off the sticky remains. As for me, I love watching them puff up and float on a sea of hot oil while turning a gorgeous golden-brown.

The batter recipe below is my Auntie Bitsa's. To carve out the balls, I use a 2-inch diameter ice cream scoop, but feel free to select another size if you prefer smaller or larger balls. As for the syrup, I love the combination of sugar, honey, and water (instead of honey only) for its smooth, scrumptious flavor. One more thing—don't worry if their shapes end up a little irregular. That's the charm of homemade.

Makes 35 balls

Walnuts

½ **cup walnut halves**

Honey Syrup

¾ **cup sugar**

¾ **cup honey**

½ **cup water**

1 **cinnamon stick**

Batter

1 **cup warm water (100 degrees, or 45-60 seconds in the microwave)**

2 **tablespoons sugar**

2 **envelopes (¼-ounce each) dry yeast**

4 **cups all-purpose flour**

1 teaspoon salt

2 cups warm water (100 degrees, or 45-60 seconds in the microwave)

7 cups vegetable oil

Ground cinnamon for topping

Paper towels

For the Walnuts: Preheat oven to 325 degrees. Place walnuts on a baking sheet and toast for 10-12 minutes. Cool 10 minutes. Chop finely; set aside.

For the Syrup: Place sugar, honey, and water in a small (1-quart) saucepan and stir with a whisk until combined well. Add cinnamon stick and cook on medium-high heat until the mixture starts to boil. Reduce to low heat and cook for 15-20 minutes without stirring; set aside.

For the Batter: Pour 1 cup warm water in a small bowl and add sugar; stir until dissolved. Add yeast, stir, and let stand 15 minutes. After the surface develops a creamy and bubbly foam you can proceed with the recipe.

Place flour and salt in a large glass or ceramic bowl. Add yeast mixture and 2 cups warm water. Stir with a whisk until combined well (the consistency will be loose and sticky). Cover bowl with a damp towel and place in a warm spot. Let stand for 1 hour until the batter doubles in size.

After one hour, poke the batter with a spatula in several places to release air. Scrape down the sides of the bowl and place near the stove.

Line 2 large baking sheets with paper towels and place near the stove.

Pour vegetable oil in a large, deep (13 x 3-inch) skillet and cook on medium-high heat until oil starts to boil. With a 2-inch-diameter ice cream scoop, carve out a scoop of batter and place in the hot oil. Repeat with the rest of the batter, being careful not to overcrowd the skillet (you will need to make 2 to 3 batches altogether). Cook about 5-7 minutes on one side, or until golden brown. Turn fritter balls over with a wire mesh spoon and cook for another 4-6 minutes, or until golden brown. Transfer to paper towels to drain.

After the fritters have drained, transfer to a serving platter. Discard the cinnamon stick from the syrup mixture and spoon the syrup over the fritter balls. Add chopped nuts and ground cinnamon; serve warm or at room temperature.

Authentic Sourdough Garlic Bread

"This is the bread which cometh down from heaven…" reads John 6:50 (KJV). This is exactly what I thought after trying my friend Michelle Tandowsky's garlic bread for the first time. "Oh, it's so easy," she said. So I figured a way to recreate it,

"Garlic bread…with real garlic!" people say while chomping a piece. Combined with an olive oil-soaked crumb, seasonings, and the freshest and most delicious sourdough loaf you can find, this recipe is simply heavenly.

Makes 1 loaf

1 to 1½-pound loaf fresh sourdough bread

8-10 cloves garlic, finely chopped (depending on loaf size)

About ½ to ¾ cup extra virgin olive oil (depending on loaf size)

Salt and freshly ground black pepper

Aluminum foil

Preheat oven to 350 degrees.

Place a sheet of aluminum foil (large enough to wrap the loaf) on a work surface.

Slice loaf in half lengthwise. Position halves side by side, cut side facing up, on top of foil.

Pour olive oil into a medium bowl and add garlic; stir to combine.

Using a 2-inch-wide pastry brush, gather olive oil and garlic and spread onto each half loaf until completely covered, including its nooks and crannies, making sure the garlic is distributed evenly. Season with salt and dash pepper. Assemble the top half over the bottom half and wrap tightly with aluminum foil.

Place in preheated oven and cook for 30 minutes. For a crunchy finish, as is pictured here, unwrap and open the bread so the halves lie side by side on top of the foil (cut side facing up). Place under a preheated broiler and cook 1-2 minutes. Using a serrated knife, slice into pieces. Place in a breadbasket and serve warm.

Vegetables – Legumes – Potatoes – Rice

(Continued)

Spinach with Rice   169

Roasted Stuffed Tomatoes with Rice   171

Roasted Summer Squash and
Onions with Feta and Mint   174

Roasted Vegetable Casserole   177

Crispy Roasted Creamer Potatoes   179

Lemon and Oregano Fingerling Potatoes   181

Orange-Glazed Sweet Potatoes   183

Rice Pilaf   185

Simple and Tasty Whole Grain Brown
or White Steamed Rice   186

Spaghetti Asparagus

Sometime ago, I watched a series on PBS, *Joanna Lumley: Greek Odyssey*, which chronicled this British actress's adventures from Athens to Southern Greece. In one of the segments, Lumley visits an old woman who lives in a deserted mountain village on the Mani peninsula in southern Greece, and learns the old woman lives mostly off the land. Fascinated by the old woman's resourceful way of life, Lumley decides to join her along the hilly terrain in search of asparagus. "Here's one," says the old woman. "There's another," points Lumley as they gather their harvest.

Afterward, they return to the old woman's tiny cottage where she prepares their just-picked asparagus with olive oil and lemon in a heavy black iron skillet. While the two women sit at the kitchen table with the feast of asparagus before them, Lumley picks up a limp one with her fingers, takes a bite, and says, "So good and so simple—like spaghetti!"

I was so enchanted by this piece that I decided to make my own version of "spaghetti asparagus." Coincidentally, the show aired in early spring when asparagus makes its short appearance in the bins. Since then, I've made this recipe many times, and each time I think of the old woman who lives in a deserted mountain village on the Mani peninsula in southern Greece.

Serves 4

1 pound asparagus

¾ cup water

¼ cup extra virgin olive oil

Salt and freshly ground black pepper

Juice from ½ lemon

Remove about 2 inches from the fibrous end of the asparagus; discard. With a vegetable peeler, peel around the stalk until just below the buds; discard peel. Rinse.

Pour water into a large (12-inch), nonstick skillet, and arrange asparagus in a single layer. Bring to a boil and cover with a large lid. Reduce heat to medium and cook for 5 minutes.

Remove lid and add olive oil, salt and pepper. With tongs, turn to coat well. Cook, uncovered, for another 4-5 minutes, or until the asparagus is limp and tender. Remove from heat and add lemon juice; toss to coat. Adjust to taste. Transfer to a plate and serve hot.

Fresh Green Bean and Tomato Stew
Fasolakia

This popular Greek vegetable dish is one of the first recipes my mother taught me. Somehow a magic wand gets waved when the versatile green bean gets married to fresh tomatoes, onions, and olive oil. Before you know it, you're filled with the spirit of the Mediterranean.

Fresh Green Bean and Tomato Stew is just as delicious served with meat, chicken, and fish as it is with a chunk of feta cheese. But before you pronounce "I do!" don't forget to douse a slice of crusty bread in the flavorful tomato sauce.

Serves 4 to 6

1 ½ pounds fresh green beans

2 large tomatoes*

¾ cup loosely packed flat-leaf (Italian) parsley, finely chopped

3 tablespoons extra virgin olive oil

1 small onion, finely chopped

Salt and freshly ground black pepper

⅓ cup dry white wine, such as Chardonnay

1 (11.5-ounce) can tomato juice*

½ teaspoon sugar

(*Note: 2 large tomatoes and 1 can tomato juice can be substituted with 1 (28-ounce) can plum tomatoes. Process canned tomatoes in a food processor for about 10 seconds.)

Trim endpoints from beans; discard. Depending on size, leave beans whole, or cut diagonally into halves or thirds. Rinse in a colander; set aside.

Peel, core, and seed the tomatoes. Chop the tomatoes coarsely; set aside.

Set aside the chopped parsley.

Place olive oil into a large (5-quart) saucepan and add onion, ½ teaspoon salt, and dash pepper. Cook on medium heat 2-3 minutes, or until onions are soft, stirring occasionally. Add chopped tomatoes, parsley, wine, ½ teaspoon salt, and dash pepper; stir until combined well. Cook for a few minutes for flavors to develop.

Add green beans, tomato juice, $\frac{1}{2}$ teaspoon salt, dash pepper, and sugar; stir until combined well. Bring to a boil. Reduce to medium-low and cook for 15 minutes, partially covered, stirring once or twice. Remove lid and continue to cook for another 10 minutes, or until beans are tender and sauce has thickened. Adjust to taste; serve hot.

Steamed Green Beans with Olive Oil, Lemon and Oregano
Fasolakia Elaiolado me Lemoni ke Rigani

Steaming is a quick and easy way to cook vegetables while still retaining their nutrients. All you need is an inexpensive metal steam basket to insert inside the pot and a little water. Here, the holy trinity of Greek cooking—olive oil, lemon and oregano—adds robust character to the mild green bean.

Serves 4

1 pound fresh green beans

2 tablespoons olive oil

1 ½ tablespoons lemon juice

1 ¼ teaspoons oregano

Salt and pepper to taste

Trim endpoints from beans; discard. Depending on size, leave beans whole or cut in half diagonally. Rinse in a colander.

Place a metal steam basket inside a medium (3-quart) saucepan and add just enough water so that it reaches the bottom of the basket. Add beans and cover. Bring to a boil and cook about 2-3 minutes, or until tender when pierced with a fork but still crisp.

Transfer beans to a serving bowl and add olive oil, lemon, oregano, salt, and pepper. Turn with a spoon to combine well. Adjust to taste; serve hot, warm, or cold.

Baked Lima Bean and Tomato Casserole
Fasolia

My mother's sister, Bitsa (short for *Haralambia*, or Harriet), was a private, quiet—yet determined—woman, and a devoted wife and mother. In addition, she had a heart for helping others, whether it was by promoting social justice or teaching the Greek language. She was also a good cook. This lima bean recipe is hers, and it's one of my favorite dishes.

Limas are rich, buttery, and sweet. Although the traditional version uses the giant ones (hence its name, Giant Beans, or *Fasolia Gigantes*), here I use the baby version instead as I find them to be more tender than their big brothers. And when combined with the luscious character of olive oil, tomatoes, onions, and garlic—well, let's just say you end up with one big, happy family.

Serves 8

1 pound baby lima beans

2½-3 pounds fresh tomatoes, or 1 (28-oz) can whole peeled tomatoes

¾ cup extra virgin olive oil

1 medium onion, finely chopped

2 cloves garlic, finely chopped

½ cup loosely packed flat-leaf (Italian) parsley, finely chopped

2 tablespoons tomato paste

1 bay leaf

1 teaspoon sugar

1½ teaspoons salt

Dash freshly ground black pepper

Advance Preparation: Place beans in a large bowl and cover with water. Let soak overnight; drain in a colander.

Fill a large (5-quart) saucepan two-thirds full of water and bring to a boil. Add drained beans and cook, uncovered, about 35 minutes, or until tender. Skim scum with a spoon and add a little water, if needed. Drain; set aside.

Peel, core, and seed the tomatoes; reserve juice. Chop tomatoes coarsely and place in a bowl. *Or,* if using canned tomatoes, place in a food processor and process 10 seconds; set aside.

Preheat oven to 400 degrees.

Pour olive oil in a large (5-quart) saucepan. Add onion and garlic and cook on medium heat until soft, about 2-3 minutes. Add chopped tomatoes and reserved juice, parsley, tomato paste, bay leaf, sugar, salt, and pepper. Stir until combined well, incorporating the paste into the mixture. Cook on medium heat, uncovered, for 8-10 minutes, stirring occasionally.

Add cooked, drained lima beans; stir to combine well. Adjust to taste.

Pour into an ungreased 9 x 9 x 2-inch baking pan and place in preheated oven. Cook for 20-25 minutes. Discard bay leaf; serve hot.

Boiled Greens
Horta

We've all been through periods when our eating habits veered off track. Whether we called it a "phase" or the more guilt-ridden "blowing it," these periods can be distressing. At first, we may not even realize something feels a little off. For example, the pleasure from eating an ice cream sundae or Big Mac can trick us into thinking all is well, and it is for just the occasional indulgence. But over time, bad habits take a toll.

I found myself in this predicament after I gave birth to our three children—within three years! I cherished being able to stay home with my little sweethearts, but unfortunately the joy of motherhood did not translate into the joy of cooking. Exhaustion was the culprit. As evidence of our plight, for a time my husband and I were changing six hundred cloth diapers per month!

Convenience started dictating many of our food choices, including the fast-food type. Where else could we take three moving targets on a shoestring budget? But as time went on, I started to not feel well. "It's your diet," they said. "You've developed food sensitivities."

Fortuitously, one day I stumbled on a book entitled *Culinaria Greece*. Instantly, I was captivated by the colorful images depicting Greece, and inspired by the simple, healthy recipes it contained. I knew I had returned home.

Immediately, I started cooking and eating healthier. And guess what? I started feeling better, too.

It's no wonder. After all, much of Greek cuisine constitutes the famous Mediterranean Diet that relies on fresh, natural ingredients: olive oil, legumes, fruits, vegetables, fish, and moderate amounts of dairy, meat, and red wine. Also considered very important are fresh herbs, like dill, thyme, mint, lavender, and oregano. As far as spices and seasonings, let's just say Greeks like to keep things simple. You won't find anything fancy or exotic in this cuisine. Instead, garlic, onions, cinnamon, lemons, salt, and pepper give this fare most of the flavor it needs.

To pay homage to the Greek diet is this beloved, nutritional side dish called *Horta* (Boiled Greens). Typically it's prepared with bitter-tasting greens like dandelion, stinging nettles, sorrel, ribwort, or wild mustard. But here, I just use the dandelion and add spinach to soften the bite—I just love the combination.

A word about dandelions: Though they can be regarded as annoying weeds, dandelion greens are regarded as one of the top-rated vegetables for their overall nutritional value. As a matter of fact, in Greece it's not unusual to see women with their kitchen knives scouring the countryside in search of them—especially after fall and spring rains.

When cooking greens, don't be alarmed by their volume. They quickly reduce to a fraction of their original size when cooked. Additionally, they need to be thoroughly cleaned of dirt particles that linger from harvest. Here, I suggest the "bucket method" (from watching my mother use her plastic wash bucket). First, trim the stems and place the greens in a bucket or any large container and cover with cold water; let stand for 15 minutes (the dirt will fall to the bottom). Then lift the greens onto a drying rack, discard the dirty water, and repeat the process one more time (that is, if you're finicky about dirt particles). The rest is easy.

My mother used to say, "One good thing leads to another good thing." So don't be surprised if, after enjoying a serving of Boiled Greens, you find more plant foods slowly creeping into your diet. And if you're like me, you'll be back to your old self in no time.

Serves 4

1 pound fresh spinach (2-3 bunches depending on size)

½ pound fresh dandelion greens (1 bunch)

3 tablespoons extra virgin olive oil

Juice from ½ lemon

Salt and freshly ground black pepper

Add water to a large (5-quart) saucepan until the level is 1-inch deep; set aside. Remove stems from spinach and dandelions and clean thoroughly (see above). Place greens inside pot and bring to a boil. Cook partially covered 3-4 minutes, or until the leaves are wilted and tender. Reserve ¼ cup of the cooked liquid; set aside. Drain the spinach in a colander. Transfer spinach to a serving bowl. Add the reserved liquid, olive oil, lemon juice, and salt and pepper; stir to combine well. Adjust to taste. Serve hot or warm.

Swiss Chard with Garlic and Lemon

Eidos Sesklou me Skordo ke Lemoni

I learned how to prepare leafy greens from my mother—the simple, healthy way. How can you go wrong with olive oil, garlic, lemon, and a little salt and pepper?

Serves 2 to 4

1 bunch Swiss chard

2 tablespoons extra virgin olive oil

2 medium cloves garlic, finely chopped

1-1½ tablespoons lemon juice (about half a lemon)

¼ teaspoon salt

Dash freshly ground black pepper

To clean the Swiss chard, trim the stalk end about 2 inches; discard. Rinse leaves well to remove dirt particles and shake off excess water. Bunch chard together on a cutting board and slice crosswise into 1-inch widths; set aside.

Place olive oil and garlic in a large (12-inch) nonstick skillet and cook on medium heat until the garlic starts to sizzle. Add sliced Swiss chard, lemon juice, salt, and pepper. Turn with tongs to coat. Cook 3-4 minutes, turning several times until leaves are wilted and tender. Adjust to taste. Transfer to a serving bowl; serve hot. (See photo on page 153.)

Tender Kale with Garlic

That kale is "in" is an understatement. But for my liking, I had to find a way to temper this esteemed green's fibrous texture and robust flavor. An ingredient tip—chicken stock—from celebrity chef Bobby Flay pointed me in the right direction, and the rest fell into place.

Serves 4 to 6

2 medium bunches kale (about 1½ pounds total)

3 tablespoons extra virgin olive oil

2 medium cloves garlic, finely chopped

1¼ cups chicken stock or broth

½ teaspoon salt

Dash freshly ground black pepper

1 tablespoon red wine vinegar

½ teaspoon sugar

Rinse kale and shake off excess water. Cut leaves away from each side of the tough, bitter stems; discard stems. In batches, bunch leaves together and slice crosswise into 1½-inch widths; set aside.

Place olive oil in a large (13 x 3-inch), nonstick deep skillet, or 5-quart saucepot. Add garlic and cook on medium heat until the garlic starts to sizzle. Add chopped kale and turn with tongs to coat. Continue to turn until kale cooks down, about 4-5 minutes.

Add chicken stock, salt, and pepper, and turn to coat. Cover and cook over medium heat another 5 minutes turning once or twice, or until the kale is tender to the bite.

Transfer kale to a serving bowl. Add vinegar and sugar and toss to combine well. Adjust to taste; serve hot or warm.

Glazed Mushrooms with White Wine

As a young girl, I would watch my mother prepare these delectable morsels and shower them over slices of roast beef for dinner. But truly, their possibilities are endless. Consider them as tasty additions to sandwiches, omelets, and rice and pasta dishes. Just make sure to remain patient toward the end of the cooking time so the mushrooms get caramelized over high heat in the reduced wine sauce. As my mother used to say, "That's where all the taste is."

Serves 4

1 ¼ pounds white button mushrooms

2 tablespoons butter

2 tablespoons extra virgin olive oil

¾ cup dry white wine, such as Chardonnay

½ teaspoon salt

Dash freshly ground black pepper

1 teaspoon finely chopped Italian parsley (optional)

To prepare the mushrooms, trim stems; discard. Lightly scrub caps under cold water to remove dirt particles and pat dry with paper towels. Depending on size, slice into halves or thirds, making sure they're all about the same size; set aside.

Place butter and olive oil in a large (12-inch) nonstick skillet and cook on medium heat until butter melts; stir fats to combine. Add mushrooms and turn with a wooden spoon or spatula to coat.

Add wine, salt, and pepper, and turn again to coat. Cook on medium heat for 8-10 minutes. Increase heat to high and cook another 6-8 minutes, stirring continuously, until the liquid evaporates and caramelized brown bits appear in the pan and around its rim. Turn the mushrooms in the caramelized bits until the mushrooms are deep golden. Transfer to a serving dish and garnish with chopped parsley; serve hot or warm.

Fresh Okra Stew with Tomatoes
Bamies Latheras me Domata

The first time I tried okra was in Greece when my *Thia* (Aunt) Ellie served it one afternoon for lunch. What was this odd, finger-shaped pod basking in rich, flavorful tomato sauce? But after a couple timid bites, I was smitten.

That would have been the end of my okra adventure had it not been for encountering it recently at a local Mediterranean restaurant. Needless to say, that same flutter returned. But this time, I decided to concoct a similar version of my own.

Okra pods arrive in the bins early summer (June and July), and range anywhere from 2 to 5 inches in length. But I prefer the shorter ones for their tender bite. Also, to get rid of okra's characteristic ooze, make sure to allow about an hour and a half of prep time before cooking (see below).

If you've never tried okra, consider embracing the new. You won't discover your passions until you do.

Serves 4 to 6

1 pound fresh okra

¾ cup red wine vinegar

3 large tomatoes

⅓ cup extra virgin olive oil

1 medium onion, sliced thinly crosswise

2-3 cloves garlic, sliced into quarters

½ cup loosely packed flat-leaf (Italian) parsley, finely chopped

Salt and freshly ground black pepper

2 tablespoons tomato paste

½ teaspoon sugar

½ cup dry white wine, such as Chardonnay

Advance Preparation: With a paring knife, trim around the conical stem and also remove the brown ring, without removing the stem itself. Place in a colander and rub each piece under running water to remove any fuzz (which is typically present in more mature okra); pat dry with paper towels. Place okra in a glass or ceramic bowl and add vinegar; toss to coat. Let stand for 1 hour, tossing 1 or 2 more times.

Meanwhile, peel, core, and seed the tomatoes. Squeeze juice through a strainer and reserve juice; set aside. Chop the tomatoes coarsely; set aside.

After 1 hour, drain the okra in a colander. Rinse well and pat dry with paper towels; set aside.

Place olive oil, onion, garlic, parsley, 1 teaspoon salt, and dash pepper in a large (5-quart) saucepan; stir to combine well. Cook on medium heat for 2-3 minutes, or until the onions are soft, stirring occasionally.

Add chopped tomatoes, reserved tomato juice, tomato paste, and sugar. Stir to combine well, incorporating paste into mixture.

Add okra and wine; stir. Bring to a boil, then reduce to medium-low heat. Cook for 45-50 minutes, uncovered, or until okra is very tender, stirring occasionally. Adjust to taste; serve hot.

Casserole-Style Spinach and Feta Cheese Pie with Phyllo
Spanakopita

My mother's recipe for this classic Greek dish is simply delicious.

Serves 12

4 bunches fresh spinach, or 4 (9-ounce) packages frozen chopped spinach

2 tablespoons butter

2 tablespoons extra virgin olive oil

1 medium onion

4 fresh green onions (scallions), finely sliced

½ cup loosely packed flat-leaf (Italian) parsley, finely chopped

Salt and freshly ground black pepper

⅓ cup dry white wine, such as Chardonnay

¼ teaspoon ground nutmeg

2 pounds feta cheese*

1 dozen eggs

1¼ cups (2½ sticks) unsalted butter

1 pound #4 phyllo (fine)

(*Note: You can substitute 2 pounds feta cheese with 1 pound feta, 1 (16-ounce) container 4% fat, small-curd cottage cheese, and 1 (8-ounce) container of ricotta cheese.)

Read Appendix A, *Being At Ease with Phyllo* (see page 321).

For the Filling: If using fresh spinach, trim stems and place leaves in a bucket or large container. Cover leaves with cold water and let stand for 15 minutes so dirt particles fall to the bottom. Lift the greens onto a drying rack, discard dirty water, and repeat the process one more time.

Add water to an extra-large (9-quart) saucepan until 1 inch deep. *(Alternatively use one large, 5-quart saucepan, and cook spinach in 2 batches.)* Add cleaned spinach leaves and bring to a boil. Cook until leaves are wilted and tender, 1-2 minutes. *Or,* if using frozen spinach, cook according to package directions.

Drain spinach in a colander using the underside of a cup or the back of a large spoon to squeeze out extra liquid. Transfer to a cutting surface and with a sharp knife cut the cooked spinach vertically and horizontally into 1-inch widths. Set aside.

In a large (5-quart) saucepan, place 2 tablespoons butter and oil. Cook over medium heat until butter melts, blending fats together. Add onion, green onions, parsley, 1 teaspoon salt, and dash pepper; stir to combine well. Continue to cook until vegetables are soft, about 3-4 minutes, stirring occasionally.

Add wine, chopped spinach, and ground nutmeg; stir to combine well. Cook on medium heat for 5 minutes, stirring occasionally. Remove from burner and tilt pot so excess liquid runs to the bottom; drain with paper towels. Set aside.

Grate feta cheese and set aside in a bowl.

Place eggs in an extra-large mixing bowl and beat on high speed for 1 minute. Add spinach mixture and cheese; stir to combine well. Set aside.

For the Phyllo: Position oven rack to second from the bottom and preheat oven to 350 degrees.

In a small saucepan, melt 1¼ cups of unsalted butter over low heat. With a pastry brush, grease a large (15½ x 10½ x 2¼-inch) baking pan with melted butter.

To form the bottom "crust," apply one sheet of phyllo to the bottom of the pan; brush completely with melted butter. Repeat 9 more times.

Add spinach mixture.

To form the top "crust," place one sheet of phyllo on top of spinach mixture and brush with melted butter. Repeat 9 more times, being sure to brush the topmost layer with butter.

Place pan in preheated oven and cook for 1 hour, or until a honey-golden color. *(Note: If the phyllo starts getting dark, cover pan loosely with aluminum foil until end of cooking time.)* Cool for 1 hour to let set. Cut into pieces with a sharp knife; serve hot.

Spinach with Rice
Spanakorizo

Aside from being suitable for Lent, this one-pot dish is a nice way to incorporate leafy greens and carbohydrates into your diet at the same time. The lemon juice at the end is like a tasty exclamation mark.

Serves 4 to 6

2 bunches fresh spinach

2 tablespoons extra virgin olive oil*

2 tablespoons butter*

1 small onion, finely chopped

1½ cups uncooked, converted, parboiled, long grain rice

2 cups chicken stock or broth

1 chicken bouillon cube, roughly chopped

Salt and freshly ground black pepper

2 tablespoons lemon juice

(*Note: For Lent, substitute 2 tablespoons olive oil and 2 tablespoons butter with ¼ cup olive oil.)

Remove stems from spinach and clean leaves thoroughly.

Add water to a large (5-quart) saucepan until 1 inch deep. Add cleaned spinach and bring to a boil. Cook for 2-3 minutes, or until wilted and tender. Drain well in a colander using the back of a large spoon or the bottom of a cup to squeeze out extra liquid. Transfer the spinach to a cutting surface. With a sharp knife, cut the drained spinach lengthwise and crosswise into 1½-inch-wide strips. Set aside.

In the same pot, add olive oil, butter, and onion. Cook on medium heat about 2-3 minutes, or until soft, stirring occasionally. Add rice; stir until combined well. Cook for 1 minute, stirring continuously. Add the chicken stock, bouillon cube, ½ teaspoon salt, and dash pepper; stir. Bring to boil. Reduce heat to medium low and cook for 10 minutes, partially covered. Add chopped spinach and stir to combine well. Cook for another 5 minutes, or until all the liquid has evaporated. Remove pot from burner and add lemon juice, stir. Adjust to taste; serve hot.

Roasted Stuffed Tomatoes with Rice
Yemistes Domates me Rizi

It was a magical summer the year I was ten. I lived with my grandparents in the Athens suburb of Palaio Faliro, and new adventures awaited at every corner. But one thing in particular took a little time getting used to.

At 6:30 a.m. I would be in deep slumber when, out of nowhere, I would be startled awake by odd screaming sounds. What's all the commotion, I wondered? It came from the street.

"Karpouzi, fresko karpouzi!" (Watermelon, fresh watermelon) one screamed.

"Domates, freskes domates!" (Tomatoes, fresh tomatoes) another hollered. Later, I would hear a wail accompanied by whinny and clop-clop sounds that I learned came from the knife grinder's horse and wagon. As it turns out, these peddlers with their pushcarts called to every window, and every housewife depended on them. Eventually I accepted these disturbances as a charming piece of Greek culture, and rolled back to sleep.

As for tomatoes here at home, it's more likely we would buy them from our local market instead of a peddler and his pushcart. But regardless, they're still an indispensable part of Greek cuisine, and are used in everything from eggs, vegetables, and salads to fish and meat dishes.

Here's a classic and cherished dish you're sure to enjoy—that is, if you're a tomato devotee like me. These plump, scarlet darlings donning their charming caps are so adorable you won't know whether to hug them or eat them. Besides, they make an attractive and flavorful accompaniment to any poultry or meat dish.

Large beefsteak tomatoes—which are in season from midsummer through early November—are ideal for this recipe because they hold their shape during roasting and allow for ample filling. As for the rice, I use an enriched, converted version—also known as parboiled—because it yields a nice, fluffy pilaf.

Yes, some things take a little time getting used to, but not this recipe.

Makes 12

12 medium beefsteak tomatoes

Extra virgin olive oil

**Salt and freshly ground
   black pepper**

1 medium onion, finely chopped

**1½ cups uncooked converted
   (parboiled) long grain white rice**

**3 chicken bouillon cubes,
   coarsely chopped**

**1 cup loosely packed flat-leaf
   (Italian) parsley leaves,
   finely chopped**

1 cup chicken stock or broth

For the Tomatoes: Grease a large (15½ x 10½ x 2¼-inch) roasting or baking pan with olive oil; set aside.

Rinse the tomatoes and pat dry with paper towels. Slice the tops off the tomatoes and place on a plate, cut side facing up. Swirl olive oil over tops and season with salt and pepper; set aside.

Core the tomatoes using a sharp paring knife; discard the cores. Starting at one-quarter to one-third-inch in, cut around the tomatoes. Gut interiors with a teaspoon, placing contents in a strainer positioned over a medium bowl. Place hollowed tomatoes in the prepared baking dish. Drizzle a little olive oil inside each tomato and season with salt and pepper; set aside.

Squeeze contents in the strainer to release juice and seeds and place drained, seeded tomato pulp on a separate plate. Reserve 1 cup of the tomato juice (discard remainder); set aside. Chop the tomato pulp coarsely until it measures about 1½ cups; set aside. Discard remaining tomato pulp, if any.

For the Rice Stuffing: Preheat oven to 425 degrees.

Pour ⅓ cup olive oil in a large (5-quart) saucepan. Add onion, 1 teaspoon salt, and dash pepper and cook over medium heat until soft, about 2-3 minutes, stirring occasionally.

Add uncooked rice and chicken bouillon and stir with a wooden spoon while crushing the bouillon pieces with the back of the spoon and incorporating them into the mixture.

Add reserved tomato juice, chopped tomato pulp, and parsley; stir. Cook over low heat for a couple minutes, stirring occasionally. Remove pot from burner and let stand a few minutes for the rice to swell.

Spoon the rice mixture into the tomato cavities until about two-thirds full.

Pour chicken broth over the rice, distributing evenly.

Place tomato tops back on the tomatoes and swirl a little olive oil over each; season with salt and pepper. Place pan inside preheated oven and roast for 40 minutes. After 40 minutes, remove tops with tongs and set aside on a plate. Reduce heat to 350 degrees and continue to cook tomatoes for another 15 minutes. Replace the tops and serve hot.

Roasted Summer Squash and Onion with Feta and Mint
Kolokythi ke Kremmydia Psito me Feta ke Menta

At the height of the season, the bountiful array of summer squash in the bins sparkles. But let's face it, served alone it can taste…well, ho-hum. So, I got to thinking about how I could turn the delicate squash into an "oh gosh!" and came up with this recipe. Adding delicious roasted onion for a hint of sweetness, feta cheese for bite, and fresh, chopped mint for pizzazz gave just the allure I needed to make this mild vegetable gleam.

Serves 4 to 6

1 large sweet onion (also called Vidalia, Walla Walla, or Maui), peeled

Extra virgin olive oil

Salt and freshly ground black pepper

2 pounds summer squash mix, such as zucchini, crookneck, and sunburst

3-4 ounces feta cheese, crumbled

8 leaves fresh mint, finely chopped

Preheat oven to 450 degrees. Grease a large (15 x 10 x 1-inch) baking sheet with 1 tablespoon olive oil; set aside.

Cut onion crosswise into ¼-inch slices and place in a single layer on prepared pan. Pour 1½-2 tablespoons olive oil into a small bowl. Dip tips of pastry brush in oil and spread on the onion slices. Season with salt and pepper. Turn over and repeat with olive oil, salt, and pepper. Place in preheated oven and cook for 15-20 minutes, or until onions have caramelized, turning over once with a spatula. Transfer to a plate and separate into rings with a fork; set aside.

Maintain oven temperature at 450 degrees and grease the same pan with another tablespoon olive oil.

Trim stems from squash, rinse and pat dry with paper towels. Cut squash so they are similar in size and density (for example, for zucchini cut crosswise into ½-inch-thick slices, and so on) and place in a bowl. Add 3-4 tablespoons olive oil and season with salt and pepper; toss to coat well. Place squash onto prepared pan, distributing in a single layer, and place in preheated oven. Cook for 15 minutes, or until underside of squash is golden brown. Turn over with a spatula and cook for another 3 minutes.

Preheat to broil and adjust the oven rack to the third level down from the top. Place separated onion rings over the squash, distributing evenly. Add crumbled feta cheese and place under broiler for 45 to 60 seconds, or until cheese melts. Add mint and serve hot, warm, or at room temperature.

Roasted Vegetable Casserole
Katsarola Lachaniko Psito

I love roasted vegetables. A high cooking temperature ensures all the moisture gets sucked right out so all that remains is sheer, dense flavor. Here, for fun, I added parsnips—carrot's mild-flavored cousin—to the colorful and nutritious assortment of late summer pickings.

Serves 4 to 6

4 medium carrots, peeled

3 medium parsnips, peeled

2 medium zucchini

⅓ pound green beans

2 medium tomatoes, cored, seeded, and roughly chopped

1 medium sweet onion (also called Vidalia, Walla Walla, or Maui)

Extra virgin olive oil

Salt and freshly ground black pepper

1 teaspoon finely chopped flat-leaf (Italian) parsley

Preheat oven to 425 degrees. Grease a large (15½ x 10½ x 2¼-inch) roasting pan with 1 tablespoon olive oil; set aside.

Make a lengthwise slit through the thick ends of the carrots and parsnips leaving the narrower portion intact. Cut crosswise into 1-inch-thick slices and place in a large bowl.

Trim ends from zucchini; discard. Rinse trimmed zucchini and pat dry with paper towels. Cut crosswise into 1-inch-thick slices; add to bowl.

Trim endpoints from green beans and cut the longer ones in half. Rinse and pat dry with paper towels; add to bowl with tomatoes.

Slice onion crosswise into ½-inch-thick slices. Separate into individual rings; add to bowl. Add ¼ cup olive oil and season with salt and pepper. Turn vegetables with a wooden spoon to coat thoroughly and pour into prepared roasting pan. Place in pre-heated oven and cook for 35-40 minutes, turning once. Adjust to taste. Add chopped parsley and serve hot.

Crispy Roasted Creamer Potatoes

These were served at my friend Michelle Tandowsky's one afternoon for a buffet lunch, and I enjoyed them so much I got inspired to make them myself. But here, I use the delicate round creamers—the baby version of the red or Yukon gold. When cooked at a high temperature, creamers retain their velvety interior texture but develop a crisp exterior bite. Plus, they make an excellent accompaniment to meat, poultry, or eggs. So next time you're hankering for a tater, give these young ones a try.

Serves 4

1 ½-2 pounds red or gold creamer potatoes

6 tablespoons extra virgin olive oil

Seasoned salt

Freshly ground black pepper

Preheat oven to 450 degrees.

Rinse potatoes and pat dry with paper towels. Cut in half crosswise or into thirds, depending on size. Place in a medium bowl. Add 2 tablespoons olive oil, seasoned salt (about ⅛ to ¼ teaspoon), and dash pepper. Turn to combine well. Repeat two more times with olive oil, seasoned salt, and pepper.

Pour into a 13 x 9 x 2-inch baking pan. Shake the pan on an even surface so the potatoes fall into a single layer. Place in preheated oven and cook for 35 minutes. Turn potatoes over with a metal spatula (they have a tendency to stick to the pan), and cook for another 5-8 minutes, or until browned on all sides. Serve hot.

Lemon and Oregano Fingerling Potatoes
Patates Lemonates

Fingerling potatoes are noted for their sweet flavor and creamy texture. These oddly charming index impostors appear in the bins either short and stubby or long and graceful. But notwithstanding their size, all possess a slight hook reminiscent of a mother scolding her young.

Here, they're prepared with olive oil, lemon, and oregano—the classic trio of Greek cuisine. So, whether you're naughty or nice, go ahead and savor these simple, delicious flavors from the Mediterranean. (Adapted from *Culinaria, Greece: Greek Specialties,* h.f. ullman, 2008.)

Serves 4 to 6

2 pounds fingerling potatoes of similar size, peeled

½ cup extra virgin olive oil

Salt and freshly ground black pepper

Dried oregano

¼ cup lemon juice

1 cup water

Preheat oven to 275 degrees.

Rinse peeled potatoes and pat dry with paper towels. Cut in half lengthwise and place in a single layer, cut side down, in a medium (15½ x 10½ x 2¼-inch) roasting pan.

Pour olive oil over potatoes and generously add oregano, salt, and pepper. Turn potatoes over and add lemon juice. Repeat with oregano, salt, and pepper. Add 1 cup water to the bottom of the pan and cover the pan tightly with aluminum foil. Place in preheated oven and cook for 45 minutes.

Remove foil and increase heat to 425 degrees. Cook for another 30 minutes, or until potatoes are golden and most of the liquid has been absorbed, adding a little extra water to the bottom of the pan, if needed. With a spatula, transfer potatoes to a plate. Adjust to taste; serve hot.

Orange-Glazed Sweet Potatoes

Not much else is needed to boost sweet potato's natural confectionery flavor, especially in today's health-conscious society. A sprinkling of olive oil, a few flecks of brown sugar, and a dash of salt is all you need.

That may well be. But during the holidays, I crave something more decadent, and return to this special recipe my Auntie Aspasia gave me years ago. Every year it's a favorite at our table. Besides, I can't think of anything else that comes close to enhancing sweet potatoes' sweetness more than lightly toasted marshmallows.

Auntie Aspasia's recipe calls for using yams or sweet potatoes, but if you're like me, you may be wondering, "What the difference?" After doing some digging, I learned these two root vegetables aren't even related. Yams have a blackish exterior and a purple or reddish interior, and are favored in Latin and Caribbean cuisine. Plus, they're generally not even available in American supermarkets.

Befuddled? According to one source, "The U.S. government has perpetuated the error of labeling sweet potatoes "yams"…[in truth] there are two types of sweet potatoes, one with creamy white flesh and one with orange, [and] the U.S. Department of Agriculture labels the orange-fleshed ones "yams" to distinguish them from the paler variety."[5]

If you're still confused, buy the ones that have the reddish skin and orange flesh (also called "red"). That is, unless you prefer the ones with light brown skin and creamy flesh (also called "jewel")!

So, give yourself permission to indulge. As my paternal grandfather used to say in Greek, *"pan metron ariston"* ("everything in moderation"), and he lived to be ninety-seven years old.

Serves 6 to 8

Butter for greasing pan

6 medium "yams" or sweet potatoes, rinsed and scrubbed

1½ cups orange juice

1½ tablespoons cornstarch

1 tablespoon grated orange zest

3 tablespoons melted butter

½ cup firmly packed light brown sugar

½ cup granulated sugar

¼ teaspoon salt

½ cup walnuts, roughly chopped

2 cups baby marshmallows

Grease the bottom and sides of a large (13 x 9 x 2½-inch) baking dish with butter; set aside.

Slice sweet potatoes in half crosswise and place in 2 large (5-quart) saucepans.

Cover with water and bring to a boil. Cook for 30 minutes, or until tender when pierced with a fork. With a slotted spoon, transfer sweet potatoes to a plate and cool about 10-15 minutes. After they have cooled, remove the skin and cut crosswise into 1-inch-thick slices. Arrange the slices in rows by overlapping the edges in the prepared baking dish, tucking the smaller pieces into the corners and empty spaces; set aside.

Preheat oven to 350 degrees.

Place orange juice and cornstarch in a small (2-quart) saucepan; stir with a whisk until combined well. Add orange zest, melted butter, brown sugar, granulated sugar, and salt; stir to combine well. Bring to a boil. Reduce heat to low and cook 3-4 minutes, or until sauce thickens. Pour over sweet potatoes and place in preheated oven. Bake for 20 minutes. Add walnuts and marshmallows over sweet potatoes, distributing evenly, and continue to cook for another 15 minutes, or until marshmallows are lightly browned. Serve hot.

Rice Pilaf
Rizi Pilafi

Here's a classic and tasty recipe for Greek rice my mother made often—and now so do I.

Serves 4 to 6

1 cup uncooked converted, parboiled, long grain rice

2 tablespoons butter

½ small onion, finely chopped

½ teaspoon salt

Dash freshly ground black pepper

2 cups water

2 chicken bouillon cubes

Place butter, onion, salt, and dash pepper in a medium (2-quart) saucepan. Cook on medium heat until onions are soft, about 2-3 minutes, stirring occasionally. Add rice; stir. Cook for about 1 minute, stirring continuously.

Add water and bouillon cubes; bring to a boil. Reduce heat to low and cook, partially covered, until all the water has been absorbed, about 15 minutes. Serve hot.

Simple and Tasty
Steamed Brown or White Rice

I can't think of a side dish more fundamental than rice—it goes with just about everything. But these days, a trip to the rice aisle at the grocery store can be dizzying. Short grain? Long grain? Whole grain? Regional? The varieties are endless.

I prefer the fluffy pile that the long grain yields. But after selecting the grain size (short or long) a myriad of other questions arise. Salt or no salt? Sticky or smooth? Oil or butter? And what about extra flavors and ingredients? The discussion is boundless.

I like to keep it simple, especially for Monday thru Friday fare. For me, the secret lies in adding just the right amount of butter and salt. I use these two recipes interchangeably. Just be mindful that the whole grain version takes 3 times longer to cook, so plan accordingly.

Serves 4 to 6

For Tasty Whole Grain Brown Rice

2 ½ cups water, or 1 ½ cups chicken stock (or broth) and 1 cup water

1 ½ tablespoons butter

1 ½ teaspoons salt

1 cup uncooked whole grain brown rice

Pour water (or stock and water combination) in a small (1 ½-quart) saucepan. Add butter and salt and bring to a boil. Add rice and stir. Reduce heat to low and cook, covered, for 45 minutes, or until all the water has been absorbed. Serve hot.

For Tasty White Rice

2 cups water

1 ½ tablespoons butter

1 ¾ teaspoons salt

1 cup uncooked long grain enriched white rice

Pour water in a small (1 ½-quart) saucepan and add butter and salt. Bring to a boil. Add rice and stir. Reduce heat to low and cook, covered, for 15 minutes, or until all the water has been absorbed. Serve hot.

Fish and Poultry

Crab Cioppino

When entertaining, blunders happen. Take the night our potluck Gourmet Club hosted New England Night, for instance. Each of us was certain our contribution to the various courses of the meal was thoughtfully considered and one-of-a kind. Well, they were one-of-a kind, all right, but all of the same food type—fish.

For appetizers we ate Cherry Tomatoes Stuffed with Smoked Oysters; Baked Clams; and Smoked Salmon Spread with Crackers. Shrimp Salad followed. And what do you think we dined on for the entrée? Fish Stew. The moral of the story? Do some fishing around before settling on a menu.

To celebrate underwater creatures everywhere, here's my mother's recipe for Crab Cioppino. The ingredients for the flavorful sauce produce a delicious bath for the medley of ocean fare. Not to mention it remains a special treat in our home just as it was when I was growing up (as evidenced by our daughter's annual request, "Mom, will you make *yiayia's* [grandma's] Crab Cioppino?"). Enjoyed with Fresh Mixed Green Salad (see page 97) and crusty sourdough bread, this dish is truly worth your time, expense, and tomato-drenched fingers!

Serves 6

Fish

2 cooked Dungeness crabs (about 4 pounds), cracked, cleaned, and crab butter removed*

2 pieces cod, or any white fish such as petrale sole, halibut, or calamari steak (about 1¼ pounds)

1 pound large prawns, peeled and deveined

¾ pound sea scallops

30 little neck clams (about 1½ pounds)

25 mussels (about ¾ pound)

(*Note: Ask the fishmonger to crack the crabs for you. Also, crab butter is the white-yellow fat inside the back shell of a large crab that many consider a delicacy.)

Tomato Sauce

½ cup extra virgin olive oil

1 medium onion, finely chopped

1 bunch fresh green onions (scallions), finely sliced

4 cloves garlic, finely chopped

4 medium ribs celery, finely chopped

4 beefsteak tomatoes, skinned, seeded and chopped, juice reserved, or 1 (28-ounce) can diced tomatoes

1 pound mushrooms, sliced

1 cup dry white wine, such as Chardonnay

Salt and freshly ground black pepper

2 tablespoons tomato paste

2 (15-ounce) cans tomato sauce

2 bay leaves

1 teaspoon dried oregano

1 teaspoon fresh thyme

½ teaspoon sugar

2 tablespoons butter

1 cup loosely packed flat-leaf (Italian) parsley, finely chopped

1 pound dry, uncooked spaghetti or angel-hair pasta, if desired

For the Fish: At home, crack the legs further with a kitchen mallet or a nutcracker so meat can be easily accessed. Discard loose shells; set aside.

Rinse the cod or white fish and pat dry with paper towels. Cut into chunks; set aside.

Rinse the prawns and scallops; pat dry and set aside.

Discard any clams and mussels whose shells are not completely closed. Place clams and mussels in separate bowls and cover with cold water. Let stand for 20 minutes to rid them of sand inside shells. After 20 minutes, lift clams and mussels out of water, discard the dirty water, and repeat this cleaning one more time. Let stand in cold water until ready to be added to the sauce.

For the Tomato Sauce: Pour the olive oil into an extra-large (9-quart) Dutch oven or stockpot. Add onion and green onions, and cook on medium-high heat. When onions start to sizzle, reduce to medium heat and cook until soft, about 3 minutes, stirring occasionally. Add garlic and cook for another minute, stirring continually.

Add celery, chopped tomatoes and reserved juice (or canned tomatoes), mushrooms, wine, 1½ teaspoons salt, and dash pepper, and stir until mixture is combined well. Bring to a boil. Reduce heat to medium and cook for 10 minutes, partially covered. Add tomato paste and incorporate into the mixture. Add tomato sauce, bay leaves, oregano, thyme, sugar, and butter. Stir until butter has melted and the mixture is combined well. Cook for 45 minutes on medium-low heat, partially covered. After 45 minutes, add parsley and continue to cook for a few more minutes. *(Note: If sauce is too thick, add ½ cup water.)*

Add crab and submerge in sauce as much as possible so the sauce can reap the full flavor of the crab. Cook for 8-10 minutes. Add sliced cod, scallops, and prawns and cook for 5 minutes.

Meanwhile, lift clams and mussels out of the water and scrub off remaining debris under running water. For the mussels, debeard (or, pull out the hairy part and discard). Pat clams and mussels dry with paper towels and add to stew. Cook about 10 minutes, or until all the shells have opened, discarding any clams and mussels whose shells did not open. Adjust sauce to taste. Serve hot over spaghetti or angel-hair pasta (cooked according to package directions), or by itself in bowls.

Simple Pan-Fried Fish with Lemon
Psari Tighanito me Lemoni

Here's an easy way to prepare any flat, white, fish. I use rice flour, which can be purchased in the flour section of most grocery stores, instead of the all-purpose kind because it yields a light, crisp crumb. Rice flour is also a welcome substitute for those sensitive to gluten.

Serves 4

4 pieces (about 1½-2 pounds) tilapia, or any flat white fish such as sole or calamari steak

1 cup rice or all-purpose flour

3 tablespoons extra virgin olive oil, plus extra if needed

3 tablespoons butter, plus extra if needed

3 tablespoons lemon juice (about 1 lemon)

Salt and freshly ground black pepper

2 teaspoons chopped flat-leaf (Italian) parsley for garnish, if desired

Rinse fish and pat dry with paper towels. Set on a plate near the stove.

Place flour in a shallow bowl and set near the stove. Dredge fish in flour and shake off excess; set aside.

Place olive oil and butter in a large (12-inch) nonstick skillet and cook on medium-high heat; blend fats together. When fats start to sizzle, place pieces of fish in skillet. *(Note: You'll probably need to make 2 batches. If so, add a little extra olive oil and butter to the pan for the second batch.)* Season with salt and pepper. Cook about 5-6 minutes, or until the underside is light golden. With a spatula, carefully turn the fish over and add lemon juice over each piece. Add salt and pepper and cook several more minutes, or until a fork can easily pierce the thickest part. Transfer to a platter and garnish with chopped parsley; serve hot.

Baked Fish Fillets with Tomatoes and Onions
Psari Plaki

Plaki is a traditional oven-cooked dish made with olive oil, tomatoes, and onions. It's often prepared during Holy Week when strict fasting rules are observed. But you don't have to be pious to enjoy my family's recipe—it's wholesome and tasty any week of the year.

Serves 4

2 pounds (about 4 pieces) white fish fillets, such as bass, cod, or halibut

Salt and freshly ground black pepper

¼ cup extra virgin olive oil

1 medium sweet onion (also called Vidalia, Walla Walla, or Maui), thinly sliced crosswise and separated into rings

1 medium clove garlic, finely chopped

3 medium beefsteak tomatoes

1 medium rib celery, finely chopped

¼ cup loosely packed flat-leaf (Italian) parsley, finely chopped

1½ tablespoons dry white wine, such as Chardonnay

2 tablespoons tomato paste

¼ teaspoon sugar

¼ teaspoon oregano

1 lemon, thinly sliced crosswise

Rinse fish and pat dry with paper towels. Place in a large (15 x 10 x 2-inch) baking pan and season with salt and pepper. Cover with plastic and set aside in the refrigerator.

Skin, core, seed, and coarsely chop the tomatoes; set tomatoes aside near the stove along with the chopped celery and parsley. Preheat oven to 350 degrees.

Add olive oil to a medium (3-quart) saucepan and add onion rings and garlic. Cook on medium heat until the onions cook down, about 5 minutes, stirring continuously so the garlic doesn't stick. Add chopped tomatoes, celery, parsley, wine, ½ teaspoon salt, and dash pepper. Stir to combine well and cook for 5 minutes, stirring occasionally.

Add tomato paste, sugar, and oregano; stir, incorporating the paste into the mixture. Cook, uncovered, about 5 minutes; adjust to taste.

Spoon the tomato mixture over each fillet. Arrange lemon slices on top and place pan in preheated oven. Place in preheated oven and cook for 20 minutes, or until a fork can easily pierce the thickest part of the fillets. Serve hot.

Baked Mediterranean Salmon

Sometimes taking a step in a new direction starts with a question.

For this recipe, I asked myself, "How can I prepare salmon with a distinct Mediterranean flavor and make it taste delicious?" But after several failed attempts, I threw my hands up and decided to just use some of my favorite, simple ingredients instead. That did it! This mild fish transformed into a dish with punch. Next time you face a similar conundrum, don't be afraid to take the plunge into the unknown. After all, how can you go wrong with passion as the common denominator?

Serves 4 or 5

Nonstick cooking spray

A 2-pound piece of salmon, skin intact

Extra virgin olive oil

Salt and freshly ground black pepper

¼ cup dry white wine, such as Chardonnay

2 tablespoons lemon juice

1 tablespoon butter, cut up in pieces

3 tablespoons julienne-cut, sun-dried tomatoes, drained

¼ cup pitted Kalamata olives (about 12), coarsely chopped

2 teaspoons fresh tarragon, coarsely chopped

2 teaspoons flat-leaf (Italian) parsley, coarsely chopped

Preheat oven to 350 degrees.

Apply a coat of nonstick cooking spray to a medium (13 x 9 x 2-inch) baking pan. Rinse salmon and pat dry with paper towels. Place in prepared pan and rub 1 tablespoon olive oil all over. Add 1 tablespoon lemon juice and season well with salt and pepper. Let stand for 15 minutes.

Pour wine, lemon juice, 1 tablespoon olive oil, ½ teaspoon salt, and dash pepper in a small bowl. Stir with a fork until combined well and pour around the bottom of the pan. Place butter pieces over salmon.

Place in preheated oven. After 10 minutes, spoon the pan liquids over the salmon and bake for another 8-10 minutes. Add the following in this order, distributing evenly: sun-dried tomatoes, chopped olives, chopped tarragon, and chopped parsley. *(Tip: This is easier to do if you take the pan out of the oven.)* Cook another 5 minutes, or until the fish can be easily pierced with a fork.

After the pan is removed from the oven, wipe down the caramelized bits with a pastry brush and incorporate with the pan liquids. Adjust to taste. Spoon pan liquids over each serving; serve hot.

Boneless Chicken Breasts with Garlic, Lemon, and Wine Sauce

At one of our favorite local restaurants, Copenhagen Bakery, my husband and I often enjoy the prawns hors d'oeuvre, not so much for the prawns themselves as for the savory sauce they're bathed in—there's never a drop left over. I thought, if it's this good on fish, why not on chicken? When I inquired, the waiter was kind enough to hint at some of the ingredients, and after some trial and error, this recipe was born.

As far as accompaniments, you may want to keep them simple, like steamed rice and broccoli. The piquant sauce has a way of awakening everything on the plate.

Next time something catches your attention, take note—maybe it's intended just for you. Once embraced, time will reveal exactly why it crossed your path. Then give a grateful nod to the universe to show you're listening.

Serves 4

Chicken

4 boneless, skinless chicken breasts*

3 tablespoons extra virgin olive oil

3 tablespoons butter

Salt and freshly ground black pepper

Sauce

2 cloves garlic, finely chopped

½ cup dry white wine, such as Chardonnay

¼ cup lemon juice

Salt and freshly ground black pepper

1 teaspoon finely chopped flat-leaf (Italian) parsley

(*Shopping Tip: It's more economical to buy chicken breasts with the bone and skin intact and to bone/skin them at home with a sharp boning knife.)

For the Chicken: Rinse breasts; pat dry with paper towels and set on a plate near the stove. Place olive oil and butter in a large (12-inch) nonstick skillet and cook on medium-high heat; blend fats together. When fats start to sizzle, add chicken and season with salt and pepper. Cook for 5-6 minutes or until the underside is light golden. Turn over and repeat. *(Note: To check for doneness, make a small slit in the thickest part of the breast to be sure the inside is white and not pink.)* Transfer to a platter.

For the Sauce: Using the same skillet, add garlic and cook on medium heat for 15 seconds, making sure it doesn't burn.

Add wine, lemon juice, 1 teaspoon salt, and dash pepper; stir. Loosen the caramel-ized brown bits on the bottom and sides of the skillet with a wooden spoon and incor-porate into the sauce. Cook 5 minutes, or until sauce reduces and thickens. Adjust to taste. Pour over chicken and add parsley; serve hot.

Broiled Chicken with Lemon and Oregano
Kota Psito me Ladolemono ke Origani

Change is tough.

When I was in the 5th grade and my father started over in the insurance business, my mother had to return to full-time employment outside the home. Although she had made arrangements for Mrs. Watry, our sitter, to be home when my brother and I arrived from school, I felt sad and lonely without my mother's warm, welcoming presence. But around this time, my role in the kitchen started to evolve. Before long, *I* was the one preparing Broiled Chicken with Lemon and Oregano or making homemade salad dressing so it would be ready for the oven when my parents came home from work.

All these years later, Broiled Chicken with Lemon and Oregano is still a regular in our home, and it's ideal for any dark meat lover. After degreasing the pan liquid, don't forget to submerge a piece of bread into the piquant sauce for extra pleasure.

The sauce also makes an excellent marinade for chicken on the outdoor grill, but be sure to let it steep in the refrigerator for at least four to six hours—or even overnight—for the flavors to soak.

Yes, change is tough, but for some reason it's part of the Plan. Over time, if you look closely enough, you may be surprised to discover a silver lining was in the making all along.

Serves 4

4 pounds dark meat chicken (legs, thighs, and wings)

⅓ cup extra virgin olive oil

⅓ cup lemon juice (1 ½-2 lemons)

Salt and freshly ground black pepper

2 ½-3 teaspoons dried oregano

Position the oven rack to third down from the top. Preheat at the broil setting.

Line a large, standard broiler pan bottom with aluminum foil to ease with cleanup. *(Note: You will not be using the vented broiler top for this recipe.)*

Trim excess fat from chicken. Trim wingtips from wings; discard. Rinse chicken pieces and pat dry with paper towels. Arrange in prepared pan. Pour half of the olive oil over chicken, then half of the lemon juice. Add half of the oregano and season generously with salt and pepper. Turn over and repeat with the remaining ingredients.

Place pan in preheated oven and cook for about 25 minutes, or until deep golden brown. With a pair of tongs, turn pieces over and cook for another 10 minutes, or until also a deep golden brown. Transfer chicken to a platter or to individual plates.

For the Sauce (if desired): Wipe caramelized brown bits from the bottom and sides of the pan with a pastry brush and incorporate into liquid. Using a fat separator, degrease and pour sauce over chicken or into individual dipping cups. Serve hot or warm.

Roasted Whole Chicken with Potatoes and Vegetables
Kota Psito me Patates ke Lahanika

It just wasn't working out.

I'm referring to the *proxenia* (matchmaking) my good-intentioned Milwaukee relatives had arranged and hoped would result in my marrying a midwestern Greek of proper social standing. I think I know why. After a while, the Steak and Brew and Brew and Steak routine that sustained our dating life became humdrum. So, when a good friend suggested that I meet "this guy who's really nice," I said yes.

On the night this guy who's really nice showed up at my door and said we were headed to an Italian restaurant in San Francisco, I livened up. On the next date, when he suggested dinner at a local Japanese restaurant, I thought hmm, he's interesting. And soon after, when I invited this guy who's really nice to my apartment for my homemade Roasted Chicken with Potatoes and Vegetables, and he responded with gratitude, I knew this nice guy named Steve was not just nice, but Mister Right.

But you don't need romance to spur making a moist, roasted, golden-brown chicken with vegetables. This classic dish suits most occasions, and is favored by all. The best part is that one large pan does all the work. Also, I like placing the bird on a roasting rack positioned in the middle of the pan because it makes for easier handling and better all-over cooking.

One final note just in case you're wondering. That old saying is true, after all—the way to a woman's heart is through her stomach.

Serves 4

Chicken

1 (4-4½ pound) whole chicken

2 tablespoons extra virgin olive oil

1 lemon cut in half

Salt and freshly ground black pepper

Vegetables

2-3 medium Yukon Gold or red potatoes

4-5 medium carrots, peeled

1 sweet onion (also called Vidalia, WallaWalla, or Maui), peeled

Salt and freshly ground black pepper

<u>Marinade</u>
¼ cup extra virgin olive oil
2 tablespoons lemon juice
1 teaspoon fresh thyme
1 teaspoon dried oregano
Salt and freshly ground black pepper
½ cup water

For the Chicken: Preheat oven to 450 degrees. Insert a roasting rack inside a large (15½ x 10½ x 2¼-inch) roasting pan. Trim excess fat from chicken and remove wingtips; discard. Rinse and pat dry with paper towels. Place on roasting rack, with the breast side down. Drizzle with 1 tablespoon olive oil and rub all over back and sides of chicken. Squeeze juice from half a lemon and season with salt and pepper. Turn chicken over and repeat; set aside.

For the Vegetables: Rinse potatoes and pat dry. Slice in half crosswise, then into quarters, then eighths. Place inside pan around the chicken. Cut carrots into 1½- to 2-inch lengths and add to pan. Slice onion crosswise into thin slices; cut slices in half. Separate the half-rings and add to pan. *(Note: Don't worry about the fullness in the pan; the vegetables cook down during cooking.)* Season vegetables with a little salt and pepper.

For the Marinade: Measure olive oil in a measuring cup. Add lemon juice, thyme, oregano, 1 teaspoon salt, and dash pepper and stir with a fork until combined well. Drizzle marinade over vegetables. Add ½ cup water to the pan and carefully turn vegetables with a rubber spatula to coat. Place in preheated oven and reduce temperature to 350 degrees. Roast for 30 minutes. Baste chicken with pan juices and cook for another 40 minutes, or until golden brown, basting 2-3 more times and turning the vegetables once or twice with a spatula.

Remove pan from oven and maintain oven temperature. Transfer the roasting rack with the chicken to a cutting board. Let it stand, using paper towels to absorb juices.

Increase oven temperature to 400 degrees. Stir the vegetables, distributing evenly around the pan. Return to oven and continue to cook for another 10-12 minutes, or until golden brown. With a slotted spoon, transfer the vegetables to a serving bowl.

Remove the roasting rack and carve chicken into slices and pieces with a carving knife. Transfer to a platter and season with salt and pepper, if desired. Serve hot alongside bowl of vegetables.

Chicken Cacciatore

My mother taught me how to make this dish many years ago, and today it's one of my family's favorites. There's just something about a long, slow simmer when braising meat on the bone that renders deep, rich character to the pot.

I like using fresh tomatoes even though preparing them requires a little work. The only problem is, locally grown tomatoes harvest mid to late summer. You say you want to make Chicken Cacciatore in mid January? Cooks everywhere face the same dilemma.

Although food critics may scoff, I maintain it isn't a sin to buy fresh produce at your local market that comes from faraway places. Nor is it sinful to reach for the canned version. Sure, you might miss the perfectly balanced, acidic-sweet tomato flavor that comes from a late August pick, but don't fret. The pleasure and satisfaction derived from those sauce-drenched smiles and finger lickin' bones will be immeasurable. Home cooking is about pleasing the heart.

Serves 6 to 8

8 chicken drumsticks and 8 chicken thighs (about 4 pounds in all), skinned

¼ cup extra virgin olive oil, plus a little extra on hand

3 tablespoons butter

1 medium onion, finely chopped

3 medium cloves, finely chopped

Salt and freshly ground black pepper

⅓ cup dry white wine, such as Chardonnay

4 large fresh tomatoes, skinned, seeded, and chopped (juice reserved), or 1 (28-ounce) can whole peeled tomatoes

½ cup loosely packed flat-leaf (Italian) parsley, finely chopped

2 tablespoons tomato paste

½ pound white button mushrooms

1 teaspoon ground cinnamon

1 teaspoon sugar

1 bay leaf

1 pound dry, uncooked spaghetti

Grated Parmesan cheese

Chopped fresh parsley for garnish (optional)

With a sharp knife, skin legs and thighs; discard skin. Rinse chicken pieces and pat dry with paper towels; set aside.

Set aside chopped fresh tomatoes and reserved juice. *Or,* if using canned tomatoes, process for 10 seconds in a food processor; set aside.

Trim stems from mushrooms; discard stems. Lightly scrub mushroom caps under cold water to remove dirt; pat dry with paper towels. Slice thinly and set aside with chopped parsley.

Place olive oil and butter in a large (13 x 3-inch) deep skillet and cook over medium heat until butter melts; blend fats together. Add onion and garlic and cook for 2-3 minutes until soft, stirring occasionally.

Add half the chicken pieces and season with salt and dash pepper. Cook over medium-high heat for about 3 minutes to brown, making sure to move the onion mixture around with a wooden spoon to prevent it from sticking. With tongs, turn chicken pieces over and season again with salt and dash pepper. Cook for another 3 minutes and transfer to a plate. Add a little more olive oil to the pan and repeat for the remaining pieces, reducing the heat slightly.

Add wine, chopped tomatoes and reserved juice (or processed tomatoes), parsley, and tomato paste to skillet. Incorporate the paste into the mixture with the back of a wooden spoon. Stir to combine well while also loosening the brown caramelized bits in the skillet and incorporating into the mixture.

Add mushrooms, ¾ teaspoon salt, dash pepper, cinnamon, sugar, and bay leaf. Stir to combine well and cook for 2-3 minutes. Add browned chicken along with accumulated juices and turn to coat/submerge in the sauce. Bring to a boil. Reduce heat to medium-low and cook, partially covered, for 20 minutes, turning once or twice. Uncover and cook for another 40 minutes, turning a couple more times. Adjust to taste.

Cook spaghetti according to package directions. Serve chicken over pasta and ladle sauce on top. Add grated cheese. Garnish with fresh chopped parsley, if desired. Serve hot.

Mexican Casserole

Marcia Signori, Ann Murphy, and I have been good friends since grade school, and we still get together regularly for lunch. One day, Marcia served this Mexican Casserole, and we loved it so much she graciously shared her recipe. I was hoping she wouldn't mind when I told her I tweaked it here and there, but she replied she did the same when she first used the recipe. By now, you can bet it bears little resemblance to the original version!

I've already made this dish countless times, and I can vouch that people of all ages love it. It's perfect for a casual Sunday supper or even a last-minute get-together with the neighbors. All you need is a simple green salad and some fresh country bread to complete the meal. But the best part is, there's little cooking time involved—the delicious harmony of ingredients does most the work.

Serves 10

1 (2-2½ pound) cooked, whole roasted chicken

1½ tablespoons butter for greasing the pan

2 tablespoons extra virgin olive oil

3 cloves garlic, finely chopped

½ medium red onion, finely chopped

½ green bell pepper, cored, seeded, and diced

½ cup loosely packed cilantro leaves or flat-leaf (Italian) parsley, finely chopped

Salt and freshly ground black pepper

1 (15½-ounce) can black beans

1 (15½-ounce) can garbanzo beans

1 (15½-ounce) can whole kernel corn

1 (16-ounce) bag shredded Mexican cheese

1 (16-ounce) container salsa, including juice

1 (15-ounce) can tomato sauce

2 heaping cups broken pieces of tortilla chips

Grease a large (15½ x 10½ x 2¼-inch) baking or roasting pan with butter; set aside.

Tear cooked chicken meat into bite-size pieces and place in an extra-large bowl.

Preheat oven to 350 degrees.

Pour olive oil into a small (8-inch) skillet. Add garlic, red onion, bell pepper, cilantro, ½ teaspoon salt, and dash pepper; stir. Cook over medium heat for 3-4 minutes until vegetables are soft, stirring occasionally. Add onion mixture to chicken.

Drain the black beans, garbanzo beans, and corn all together in a colander. Add to chicken.

Add the cheese, salsa, tomato sauce, tortilla chips, 2 teaspoons salt, and ½ teaspoon pepper to chicken. Mix thoroughly until combined well. Pour mixture into prepared pan and place in preheated oven. Cook for 20-25 minutes; serve hot.

Baked Turkey Breast with White Wine

When I was young, my mother would occasionally heat up a Swanson frozen dinner when she was in a pinch. Called TV dinners, my favorite came with roast turkey, stuffing, corn, and a puddle of gravy that sat in a large thumblike indentation atop the mashed potatoes. Needless to say, I loved every morsel. But eventually, my mother taught herself how to prepare the real thing. Years later, when I bemoaned what to cook that night for my family, she suggested I make her turkey breast recipe. "It's easy and so good," she said.

As was usually the case, Mom was right. Here, caramelized bits from the pan get incorporated into the sauce to add tasty flavor to the moist, tender meat. My husband says, "Every time I eat this, I feel so healthy." Maybe so, but I sure wouldn't mind another bite of that Swanson's.

Serves 4

1 half turkey breast*, 2½ to 3 pounds

2 tablespoons extra virgin olive oil

Salt and freshly ground black pepper

1 tablespoon butter, cut up in pieces

1 cup dry white wine, such as Chardonnay

½ cup water

(*Note: Turkey breasts are commonly sold whole, so ask the butcher to cut one in half for you.)

Preheat oven to 325 degrees.

Trim excess fat from turkey breast; discard. Rinse breast and pat dry with paper towels. Place in a medium (13 x 9 x 2-inch) baking pan, breast side down. Drizzle 1 tablespoon olive oil and rub all over. Generously add salt and pepper. Turn breast over and repeat. Place butter pieces on the top. Add ¾ cup wine and ¼ cup water to the bottom of the pan.

Place pan in a preheated oven and cook for 45 minutes, basting every 15 minutes with pan juices. Add the remaining ¼ cup wine and ¼ cup water to the bottom of the pan (or a little more, if needed), and cook for another 25 minutes, or until the thickest part of the meat is white and not pink, basting one or two more times,

Transfer breast to a carving board and let stand for 5 minutes. Meanwhile, wipe down the caramelized brown bits around the sides and bottom of the pan with a pastry brush and incorporate with the pan liquid. Using a fat separator, degrease; set aside.

Carve the meat into slices and transfer to a serving platter. Pour degreased sauce over meat and season with salt and pepper to taste; serve hot.

Meats

Easy Sirloin Tip Roast

My favorite dinner as a kid was sliced roast beef with a baked potato, green salad, and a slice of warm, crusty French bread slathered with butter. That meal reminds me of the time we were a family—when Dad sat at one end of our brown laminate kitchen table, me opposite, my brother to my right, and my mother to the left. I wasn't aware of being grateful then, but I was conscious of all those tight feelings, like when a sponge gets squeezed. Before long, my family would crumble—my parents would divorce and my brother become estranged. Even the four-bedroom ranch home with that brown laminate kitchen table would be gone. On the other hand, my mother and I remained nuclear, and each clung to the other dearly.

But these experiences have a way of stretching us, like the folding, pressing, and stretching motions when kneading dough. How else does one achieve a beautifully risen loaf of freshly baked bread? The way yeast ferments bread, so do pleasures and pangs enrich the character of the human heart.

I wasn't aware of being grateful then, but I am now. For that plate of roast beef; for my parents and the unexpected occasions toward the end of their lives to witness their love for each other—a gift that brought me peace and fulfillment beyond measure; and finally, for the memory of the four of us seated around that brown table.

*

My mother's recipe for roast beef uses the economical tip from the bottom sirloin (versus the top sirloin, where sirloin steaks come from). You can buy the full size that weighs 5 to 6 pounds and serves 10 to 12 people, or the half cut, described below. A meat thermometer is crucial to gauging the desired level of doneness, but be sure to remove the meat from the oven just *before* the desired level of doneness, as it continues to cook while it rests.

Serves 6

1 (2½-3-pound) sirloin tip roast

2 tablespoons extra virgin olive oil

Salt and freshly ground black pepper

1½ tablespoons butter, cut up in pieces

¾ cup dry white wine, such as Chardonnay, plus a little extra if needed

¼ cup water, plus a little extra if needed

Preheat oven to 350 degrees.

Rinse meat and pat dry with paper towels. Leaving the strings intact, place in a medium (12 x 9 x 1¾-inch) pan. Pour 1 tablespoon olive oil over the meat and rub all over the top and sides. Generously season with salt and pepper. Turn over and repeat.

With the fat side up, arrange the butter pieces over the meat. Add ½ cup of the wine and 3 tablespoons of the water to the bottom of the pan. Insert a meat thermometer into the thickest part, pressing it all the way until it touches the bottom of the pan. Place in preheated oven and cook for 30 minutes.

After the meat has cooked 30 minutes, add the remaining ¼ cup wine and 1 tablespoon water. With a pastry brush, loosen the caramelized brown bits from the sides and bottom of the pan and incorporate into the liquids. *(Note: If needed, add a little more wine and water to the pan.)* Cook until just before desired level of doneness. Transfer meat to a cutting board to rest about 5 minutes.

Remove the thermometer. Cut strings; discard. Carve meat into thin slices, absorbing runny juices with paper towels; transfer to a serving platter.

Loosen remaining caramelized bits in the pan and incorporate with liquids. Using a fat separator, degrease the pan liquid and pour over the meat slices. Adjust to taste with salt and pepper; serve hot.

Veal Stew with Leeks and Carrots
Moskhari me Prasa ke Karotta

I don't cook veal often, so when I do it's a treat. This recipe especially appealed to me because of its nifty one-pot approach. No doubt the onion, leeks, celery, and herbs add a solid nutritional component to this dish, but it's the lowly carrot—usurping with brilliance ascribed to jewels—that cajoles. At the end, lemon juice adds sturdy bite.

While the ingredients take their cue from the original version I found in a cookbook, I rewrote the method for clarity. Home cooks are all too familiar with the confusion, frustration, and panic that arise with murky instructions. It's like getting lost on the way to your destination. Did I miss a turn? Which way now? Right? Left? Conversely, a clear and concisely written recipe makes straight our path. (Adapted from *Culinaria Greece: Greek Specialties*, h.f.ullmann, 2008.)

Serves 4 to 6

2-2½ pounds veal stew meat

⅓ cup extra virgin olive oil

**Salt and freshly ground
  black pepper**

1 medium onion, finely chopped

**2 medium ribs celery,
  finely chopped**

**1 cup dry white wine, such as
  Chardonnay**

½ cup chicken stock or broth

2 bay leaves

2 leeks

4 medium carrots

¾ cup chicken stock

2 egg yolks

**3 tablespoons lemon juice
  (1-2 lemons)**

2 teaspoons cornstarch

**½ cup loosely packed flat-leaf
  (Italian) parsley, finely chopped**

Pour olive oil in a large (5-quart) saucepan or Dutch oven and turn heat to medium-high. When the oil gets very hot, add the veal in batches, being careful not to overcrowd the pan. Season with salt and pepper and cook 4 minutes on each side, or until browned. Transfer to a plate; set aside.

Add onion and celery to the same pot and cook on medium heat for about 1 minute, stirring a few times. Add wine and ½ cup stock or broth and stir while incorporating all the caramelized bits from the pot into the liquid. Cook 5 minutes.

Add browned meat and accumulated juices, bay leaves, ½ teaspoon salt, and dash

pepper; stir to combine well. Bring to a boil. Reduce heat to medium-low and cook for 50 minutes, partially covered, or until the meat is tender, stirring occasionally.

Meanwhile, prepare leeks and carrots. For the leeks, slice off root ends, green tops, and tough outer leaves; discard. Make a lengthwise slit and fan under cold water to remove dirt particles. Slice leeks into 1-inch lengths and set aside on a plate near the stove. For the carrots, peel and cut diagonally into $1\frac{1}{2}$-inch lengths, making a lengthwise slit at the root end if too thick. Set aside on a plate near the leeks.

After the veal has cooked for 50 minutes, add the chopped leeks, carrots, and $\frac{3}{4}$ cup chicken stock or broth; stir to combine well. Bring to a boil. Reduce heat to medium-low and cook for another 45 minutes.

Meanwhile, prepare egg yolk mixture. Place egg yolks in a small bowl and add lemon juice and cornstarch. Stir with a fork until smooth and evenly blended.

After the veal has cooked for 45 minutes, add the egg yolk mixture and chopped parsley; stir to combine well. Cook for 1-2 minutes, or until sauce thickens. Adjust to taste and serve hot.

Traditional Roast Leg of Lamb with Potatoes
Arni Psito me Patates

Essence (noun): the basic nature of a thing; the quality or qualities that make a thing what it is.[6]

I'm referring to certain idiosyncrasies concerning Greek dining life.

For that summer in Greece between high school and college, there were many times I had to remain quiet at the dinner table. Mind you, not for any lack of desire to be social, but because I was unable to understand and speak the language fluently. In short, I was forced to observe. But what I saw and heard may well have been the best entertainment in the categories of comedy and drama I've ever experienced.

To begin with, every swallow was accompanied by animated discussions about politics, business, family, or whatever ridiculous point while emotions burst forth like fireworks on the Fourth of July. Aided by physical gestures like flailing arms, talking hands, bobbing shoulders, and moving torsos, you knew something poignant was being said. This was most of the time. Let's just sum it up by saying Greeks are a lively sort.

In addition, I was captivated by the way they manipulated their utensils. To illustrate, the right hand would hold the knife while the left, the fork. Then the knife would make various gliding motions assisting the fork in whatever it needed—a little extra sauce, a slight lift, or a gentle cut. So graceful and refined was this interplay between knife and fork that it resembled a beautifully choreographed ballet.

In contrast, the right hand often performed solo by piercing a *mezede* (appetizer) with a fork using a thumb and index finger contorted in a way that could only be described as *European*. And when combined with impassioned gusto, these stellar acts made me conclude that, in addition to philosophical thought and pleasing architecture, the Greeks invented multitasking.

If this describes the essence of how they eat, what could possibly depict the lifeblood of what they eat more than roasted lamb? At Greek festivals and Easter picnics, many have stood in awe at the familiar sight of a whole lamb being roasted over an open-flame fire pit. But inside the home, Traditional Roast Leg of Lamb with Potatoes triumphs.

As for preparing a leg of lamb, it's helpful to know this cut has built-in tenderness and great flavor. So why not just throw in a few potatoes, put it in the oven, and walk away? I wish it were that easy.

While the ingredient list below is simple, roasting a leg of lamb with potatoes is a dance with oven temperature, the interior temperature of the meat, and the level of liquid in the pan—all of which require an alert eye. So does determining the right time to take the roast out of the oven. Although the general rule is 15 minutes per pound for rare, 20 for medum-rare, 25 for medium, and 30 for well-done, a few deep pokes along the way from an instant-read thermometer are indispensable for communicating what's actually going on inside—I couldn't do without mine.

For the potatoes, attentiveness to the level of liquid in the pan—adding more wine and water as needed, and increasing the temperature at the very end—ensures a flavorful, crusty-brown finish. In the end, a recipe is merely a set of instructions—trust your instincts.

Serves 6

1 (5 to 7½-pound) leg of lamb*

5-6 whole cloves garlic, peeled

Extra virgin olive oil

Salt and freshly ground black pepper

Dried oregano

Water

10 small, unpeeled red potatoes (about 2½ pounds)

2 cups dry white wine, such as Chardonnay, plus extra on hand

(*Note: Ask your butcher to crack the bone for you, if possible. This eases placement inside the pan.)

Remove lamb from refrigerator 1 hour before and let stand.

Preheat oven to 450 degrees.

Trim excess fat from lamb with a sharp knife; discard. Rinse lamb and pat dry with paper towels. Position a roasting rack inside a large (15¾ x 12 x 2¾-inch) roasting pan. Place the lamb on the rack, bone side up. Make 2 or 3 deep slits (anywhere, but placed apart) with a sharp knife and insert that number of garlic cloves inside the slits. Drizzle lamb with olive oil and rub all over. Add the following generously, one at a time: salt, pepper, and oregano.

Turn lamb over. Make 3 more deep slits and insert remaining garlic cloves. Repeat with olive oil, salt, pepper, and oregano. Add 1½ cups water to the bottom of the pan; set aside.

For the potatoes, rinse and pat dry with paper towels. Cut in half crosswise and place in a bowl. Generously drizzle olive oil over the potatoes and turn to coat. Generously add salt, pepper, and oregano and turn to combine well; set aside.

Place pan in preheated oven and cook for 10 minutes. Reduce heat to 325 degrees. Add prepared potatoes (you can remove pan from the oven to do this if you prefer) and pour 2 cups wine and $\frac{1}{2}$ cup water over the potatoes; turn with a spatula to coat. Cook for $1\frac{1}{2}$ hours, or until just before the meat reaches the desired level of doneness* according to an instant-read thermometer. While the meat is cooking, turn the potatoes 2 or 3 times, adding more wine and water (about $\frac{1}{2}$ cup at a time) as needed when pan liquid gets low.

(*Note: The general rule of thumb for doneness is 125 degrees for rare [not very tender and still bloody]), 130-135 degrees for medium-rare [tender but still pink]), 135-140 degrees for medium [tender], or 155-160 for well-done.)

After the meat is cooked, transfer to a cutting board. Let rest for 10-15 minutes. *(Note: The meat continues to cook while it rests.)*

Meanwhile, increase oven heat to 400 degrees. While the pan is still out of the oven, add a little water (about $\frac{1}{3}$ cup or as needed), and with a pastry brush, wipe down all the caramelized brown bits on the bottom and sides of the pan and incorporate with liquid. Turn potatoes to coat and return pan to oven. Cook for 10-15 minutes, or until potatoes get browned and crusty. Transfer potatoes to a serving dish.

Carve meat into slices and season with salt and pepper. Serve warm alongside the potatoes.

Simple Broiled Lamb Chops
Paidakia

Even the tiniest food details impressed me as a child. For example, one evening in Athens, my *yiayia* (grandmother) served lamb chops for dinner with a half a lemon on each plate. What's that for, I wondered? I watched as my *yiayia* and mother squeezed the juice over the meat, and timidly mimicked their act. I loved the combination of flavors! From then on, I craved a dash of tang along with my lamb.

But then again, I'm a sucker for lamb chops.

The rib loin ones come from the prime and distinguished rib loin section—the tastiest part of the animal. But despite its regal location, when it comes to eating these little darlings the courteous fork and knife method simply doesn't work for me. Instead, I like to get my fingers dirty. How else can one savor all the flavorful bits around the heel of the chop and shaft without making a real go of it? Honestly, this is no time to withhold such pleasure.

Serves 4

8-12 rib loin lamb chops

Salt and freshly ground black pepper

Dried oregano

Preheat oven to broil setting; position oven rack to the third level down from the heating unit.

Line the bottom of a large broiling pan with aluminum foil (to aid with cleanup). Place the vented broiler on top.

Place chops on the vented broiler top. Generously add salt, pepper, and oregano. Turn over and repeat. Place pan in preheated oven and cook for 6-8 minutes (*Note: Due to a number of factors, the cooking time may vary. You want to make sure the fatty edges are starting to get golden brown and crisp before turning over to the other side.*) Turn over with a fork and cook for another 3-4 minutes, or until done. Serve hot.

Lamb Tajine with Olives

I didn't know a thing about Moroccan food and culture, but when it came my turn to host one of our Gourmet Club dinners, I chose that as our theme. Why not? At the very least, it sounded exotic and intriguing.

After doing some research, I came upon this recipe, and knew the main entrée could be checked off my to-do list. Needless to say, it's been part of my treasured collection of recipes ever since.

This stew is traditionally slow-cooked in a North African tajine, or clay pot, but instead, I use a covered braising pan (a Dutch oven works well, too). I love the medley of spices with its deep autumnal tones. Not only does it create a feast for the palate, but for the eyes as well. Olives add Mediterranean spirit, but this time from the other side of the Sea.

Now that the theme and entree were decided, how was I going to create ambience apropos for ten people (five members plus our charter-mandated dates) in my tiny studio apartment on a shoestring budget?

I decided to take my cue from the desert-dwelling Bedouins. We dined nomadic-style, on a large bedspread placed on my living room floor. With all incandescence turned off, candlelight flickered everywhere while clouds of incense traveled the air. We ate with our hands, drank, and laughed while traditional Berber folk music played in the background. Who would have thought taking a chance on the unknown could be so much fun? It was truly a memorable evening. (Recipe adapted, source unknown.)

Serves 4 to 6

3½ pounds lamb shoulder chops

⅓ cup extra virgin olive oil, plus a little extra on hand

1 medium onion, finely chopped

3 cloves garlic, finely chopped

1 teaspoon ground ginger

1 teaspoon paprika

¼ teaspoon ground cumin

¼ teaspoon ground turmeric

Salt and freshly ground black pepper

1 cup water

¾ cup finely chopped fresh green onions (scallions), about 5

½ cup loosely packed flat-leaf (Italian) parsley, finely chopped

1 (15-ounce) can tomato sauce

¼ cup lemon juice, about 1 lemon

1 cup black or green pitted Mediterranean olives

Rinse chops; pat dry with paper towels. Trim excess fat and discard. Cut each chop vertically down the middle (where there is no bone). Where you are able (where there is no bone), cut meat horizontally or diagonally into large chunks; set aside.

Pour ⅓ cup olive oil in a large (13-inch) heavy-bottomed, covered braising pan or large Dutch oven. Add onion and garlic and cook on medium heat until soft, about 2-3 minutes, stirring occasionally.

Add meat, ginger, paprika, cumin, turmeric, 1 teaspoon salt, and dash pepper and turn lamb to coat well. Increase heat to medium-high and cook 8-10 minutes on one side until browned. Turn meat over with tongs and add a little extra olive oil. Brown this side about 5 minutes, while stirring the onion and spice mixture continuously so it doesn't stick. Add water and incorporate liquid with the onion and spices. When liquid comes to a boil, reduce to low heat. With the back of a wooden spoon, release all the caramelized brown bits on the sides and bottom of the pan and incorporate into the liquid. Cook for 1 hour, partially covered, stirring occasionally. Turn meat once or twice.

After the meat has cooked 1 hour, add green onions, parsley, tomato sauce and lemon; stir to combine well. Increase heat slightly and cook for another 10 minutes, partially covered.

Add olives; stir. Adjust to taste. Remove from heat and let stand for 5 minutes. Serve hot with Tasty White Steamed Rice (see page 186).

Lamb and Vegetable Stew
Arni me Lahanika

My mother grew up in the historic Koukaki district of Athens just blocks from a 2,500-year-old stone wonder called the Acropolis. "I walked to school every day, and all I had to do was look up—there it was," she would say to me. About her childhood my mother added, "We didn't have a lot of money, but our lives were so simple and content."

She continued, "My family and I would sing folk songs, like *Yirise* (Come Back to Me), *Samiotisa* (Girl from the Island of Samos), or *Ti Omorfi Pou Ise Otan Kles* (How Beautiful You Look When You Are Crying) in beautiful harmony. And name days (feast days of the year that honor the saint associated with one's Christian name) never passed without a celebration. For example, we used to go to *Thio* (Uncle) Dino's home every year on his name day and *Thia* (Aunt) Eleni would make lamb stew."

Years later, my mother mastered the lamb stew, and this braised, falling-off-the-bone delicious dish became my father's favorite. Long after they divorced, I continued making it for him, especially on Christmas Eve when he sat at our table as our honored guest. Need I mention that Dad loved drenching warm, crusty bread in its rich tomato sauce? How could a Greek not?

As a matter of fact, fresh white (and as of recent years whole wheat, too) crusty bread is an indispensable part of any Greek meal. As far as their craft of sopping, I haven't any doubt it rivals no other. This fact became evident one summer I visited Greece.

There, a small piece was torn from a slice of bread and submerged in sauce or salad dressing where it would sit for five to ten seconds until drenched before being consumed. Alternatively, a fragment of bread could get dabbed gently, like a lady touching up her face powder. But regardless, the inevitable long sweeping motions at the end of a meal rendering one's plate spotless—a gesture representing the highest compliment given a cook—always resulted in a sated stomach and a meal truly enjoyed.

I still remember my father's delight in eating a plate of lamb stew, and the fulfillment I received as the cook. These simple pleasures and memories are grand—perhaps even as grand as the mighty Acropolis.

Makes 6 Servings

6 lamb shoulder chops (about 4-4½ pounds)

Salt and freshly ground black pepper

⅓ cup extra virgin olive oil

1 medium onion, finely chopped

3 medium cloves garlic, finely chopped

1 cup water

1 tablespoon all-purpose flour

½ cup dry white wine, such as Chardonnay

2 bay leaves

4 thick carrots, peeled

4 thick zucchini

4 medium ribs celery

4 medium red potatoes

½ cup water

2 tablespoons tomato paste

2 (11.5-ounce) cans tomato juice

1 teaspoon ground cinnamon

1 teaspoon sugar

Rinse chops and pat dry with paper towels. Cut chops vertically through the center and trim excess fat; discard.

Pour olive oil in an extra large (9-quart) Dutch oven and heat on medium-high. When oil is very hot, add lamb pieces and brown (you will need to brown the meat in 2 batches), being careful not to overcrowd the pan. Season with salt and pepper and cook for 5 minutes. With a pair of tongs, turn meat over and season again with salt and pepper; cook about 4 minutes. Transfer to a plate; set aside. Turn off heat and pull pot away from burner.

Measure 1 cup water and add flour; stir with a whisk or fork until smooth; set aside.

Add onion and garlic to same pot and cook on medium-low heat for 2-3 minutes, stirring occasionally. Add wine and stir, incorporating all the caramelized brown bits into the liquid. Add browned meat and accumulated juices.

Add water and flour mixture to meat. Add bay leaves and stir to combine well. Bring liquids to a boil. Reduce to low heat and cook for 1 hour, partially covered, turning the meat every 10-15 minutes.

Meanwhile, prepare the vegetables. Trim ends from carrots, celery, and zucchini; discard. Rinse and pat dry with paper towels. Cut diagonally into 1½-inch thickness; set aside in the refrigerator until ready to use.

Measure ½ cup water and add tomato paste; stir until smooth.

Rinse potatoes and pat dry. Cut in half crosswise, then into quarters, then eighths.

After the meat has cooked for 1 hour, add the tomato paste mixture, tomato juice, carrots, celery, zucchini, potatoes, cinnamon, sugar, 1½ teaspoons salt, and dash pepper. Turn to coat the vegetables and meat and stir the liquids to combine well. Bring to a boil. Reduce heat to medium-low and cook for 1 hour, partially covered, stirring the liquid and turning the vegetables and meat every so often. Adjust to taste; serve hot.

Jambalaya

I was inspired to create my own version of this classic southern favorite after ordering it one day in a restaurant. Besides, just say "one pot" and I get a soft spot! Magically, these meals taste even better the next day after the flavors have had a chance to be absorbed.

I love the salty flavor of pork sausages. Here, caramelized bits rendered in the pot from browning them furnish this dish's savory essence. All you need is a green salad to complete the meal.

Serves 6 to 8

½ pound dried kidney beans, soaked overnight

12 uncooked pork sausage links, about 1 ¼ pounds

2 tablespoons butter

1 medium onion, finely chopped

2 medium ribs celery, finely chopped

½ medium green bell pepper, diced

1 cup loosely packed flat-leaf (Italian) parsley, finely chopped

1 (28-ounce) can diced tomatoes, including juice

2 tablespoons tomato paste

1 ½ cups uncooked converted long grain rice

1 (14.5-ounce) can chicken broth

1 cup water

2 chicken bouillon cubes, coarsely chopped

1 teaspoon salt

Dash freshly ground black pepper

½ teaspoon sugar

¼ teaspoon hot pepper sauce

Advance Preparation: Place kidney beans in a large bowl and cover with water. Let soak overnight. Drain in a colander.

Fill a large (5-quart) saucepan about two-thirds full with water and bring to a boil. Add beans and cook 20-25 minutes, or until tender. Drain in a colander; set aside.

[]

Wipe pot to reuse for the remainder of the recipe.

Place sausage links in the same saucepan and cook until browned on all sides, about 20 minutes in all; transfer to paper towels to drain. Reserve 1 tablespoon of sausage fat and set aside. Discard the remaining fat.

Place sausage on cutting board and cut into ½-inch widths; set aside.

Place reserved pork fat, butter, and onion in the pot and cook on medium heat until soft, about 2-3 minutes, releasing the caramelized brown bits with a wooden spoon and incorporating into the mixture. Add celery, green bell pepper, parsley, diced tomatoes (including juice), and tomato paste. Incorporate the paste into the mixture, and stir to combine ingredients well.

Add uncooked rice, chicken broth, 1 cup water, bouillon cubes, 1 teaspoon salt, dash pepper, sugar, and hot pepper sauce; stir to combine well. Bring to a boil. Reduce heat to medium-low and cook, partially covered for 20 minutes. Add cooked sausage and beans; stir to combine. Continue to cook, uncovered, for another 5-10 minutes, or until all the liquid has evaporated. Adjust to taste; serve hot.

Moussaka

Summer, 1975. Athens, Greece

One afternoon, my cousin Angela took me to meet her future mother-in-law, Mrs. Dritsas. When we arrived, a short, round woman with blackish-gray hair pulled back in a bun, wearing a print dress, black leather lace-up shoes, and not a drop of makeup, warmly welcomed us inside her tiny apartment. Right away she swept us into her even more minuscule, dimly lit kitchen. "Please sit down and stay for lunch. I just made moussaka," she said.

I watched as Mrs. Dritsas cut and served us each a large piece. At first, I didn't know whether to start eating or simply enjoy its luscious appearance. But seduced by thick layers of eggplant, potato, meat, and dribbles of rich olive oil, I was overcome with its deliciousness after the first bite—wow! Needless to say, nary a bite remained on my plate.

To this day, I still think about Mrs. Dritsas's moussaka, and the humble woman who generously shared her gifts of hospitality and fine cooking. There's no lasting importance in designer clothes, luxury homes, remodeled kitchens, and high-end appliances, but there is in sharing our gifts with others. And she did that.

Admittedly, I consider my mother's potato-less version of this traditional Greek dish to be on par with that memorable one. To vouch for its exquisiteness, when I prepared this recipe for a couple of my college girlfriends, one commented, "This is a $300,000 recipe," but I'll let you be the judge.

And finally, because moussaka takes time to prepare, consider breaking the job up into timesaving steps. For example, I prefer to roast the vegetables and arrange them in the pan the night before. But if you'd rather cook it in one fell swoop, *bravo sas* (bravo to you)!

Serves 12

<u>Eggplants and Zucchini</u> (bottom layer)

3 large eggplants

8 medium zucchini

Extra virgin olive oil

Salt and freshly ground black pepper

<u>Meat</u> (middle layer)

2 pounds ground beef

¼ cup extra virgin olive oil

1 medium onion, finely chopped

4 medium cloves garlic, finely chopped

½ cup dry white wine, such as Chardonnay

1 bunch fresh green onions (scallions), finely chopped

1 cup loosely packed flat-leaf (Italian) parsley, finely chopped

Salt and freshly ground black pepper

1 (15-ounce) can tomato sauce

1¼ teaspoons ground cinnamon

½ teaspoon sugar

<u>Béchamel and Cheese Sauce</u> (Mornay) (top layer)

2 cups grated Monterey Jack cheese

½ cup grated Parmesan cheese

2 cups whole or 2% low-fat milk, plus ¾ cup reserved if needed

½ cup (1 stick) butter

1 cup all-purpose flour, sifted

¼ teaspoon salt

4 egg whites

2 egg yolks

Preheat oven to 425 degrees. Grease a large (14¾ x 10¾ x 2¼-inch) baking pan with olive oil; set aside.

For the Eggplants: Grease 2-3 large nonstick (preferred) baking sheets with olive oil. Trim ends from eggplants and cut into ¾-inch-thick slices. With a paring knife, remove peel; discard peel. Place sliced eggplants on prepared baking sheets. Measure ¾ cup olive oil (or a little more if needed). Dip the ends of a pastry brush in the olive oil and wipe the top and sides of the eggplant; season with salt and pepper. Turn over and repeat.

Place pans in preheated oven and cook for 15 minutes, or until side facing down is golden brown. Turn over and continue to cook for another 10 minutes, or until the other side is also golden brown. Transfer the eggplant to the prepared baking pan with a spatula and arrange by slightly overlapping the edges.

For the Zucchini: Preheat oven to 450 degrees. Grease the same baking sheets again with olive oil. Trim ends from zucchini, rinse, and pat dry with paper towels. Slice in half lengthwise and place on the prepared baking sheets. Measure ⅓ cup olive oil (or a little more if needed) and brush the tops with the oil; season with salt and pepper. Turn over and repeat.

Place in preheated oven and cook 18-20 minutes, or until side facing down is golden brown. Turn over and cook for another 8 minutes, or until the other side is also golden brown and the zucchini is tender all the way through when pierced. Arrange zucchini over the eggplant with a spatula, distributing evenly. Set aside.

For the Meat: Break up meat into small pieces and place in a large (5-quart) saucepan. Brown over medium heat; drain fat. Transfer to a plate; set aside. Wipe the pot for next use.

In the same pot, pour ¼ cup olive oil and add onion and garlic. Cook over medium heat for 2-3 minutes, or until soft, stirring occasionally. Add wine, green onions, parsley, 1 teaspoon salt, and dash pepper; stir until combined well. Cook over medium heat for a few minutes for the flavors to develop. Add cooked meat and stir until combined well. Add tomato sauce, cinnamon, 1 teaspoon salt, dash pepper, and sugar; stir until combined well. Cook the mixture over medium-low heat for 5-10 minutes, or until it thickens. Adjust to taste. Spoon meat mixture over the roasted vegetables and smooth evenly; set aside.

For the Béchamel and Cheese Sauce: Set aside an extra-large mixing bowl for later use.

Place Monterey Jack and Parmesan cheeses and the reserved milk near the stove.

Place 2 cups cold milk in a medium bowl. Gradually add flour and stir with a whisk until mixture is smooth; set near stove. *(Note: This is not the traditional method for making béchamel, but it works well with this recipe.)*

Melt butter in a large (5-quart) saucepan. Over medium-low heat, slowly add milk mixture, stirring with a whisk continuously. Add cheeses and salt and continue to stir until cheeses are almost melted. Remove from heat. Add ¼ cup reserved milk; stir. *(Note: The mixture should be gummy but workable when stirring. If too gummy, add another ¼ cup of milk [or a little more, if needed] up to no more than ¾ cup in all.)* Pour into extra-large bowl and let cool about 20 minutes, stirring a couple times to release steam.

Preheat oven to 350 degrees.

After the milk mixture has cooled, place 4 egg whites in a medium bowl and 2 egg yolks in a small bowl. With a portable electric mixer, beat the egg whites until stiff. Beat the yolks until creamy. Add the yolks to the whites and blend on low speed until combined well.

Fold* the eggs into the milk mixture until smooth and uniform. Pour over the meat mixture and place in preheated oven. Bake for 45 minutes, or until golden brown. Cool for at least 30 minutes to 1 hour for the sauce to set. Serve hot.

(*Note: To fold in the eggs, "cut" the mixture in half vertically with a spatula, bring the spatula down and across the bottom of the bowl, and then turn it over into the mixture. Keep repeating until you achieve an even blend.)

Phyllo-Wrapped Meat Rolls with Béchamel and Cheese Sauce
Bourekakia me Kreas

My mother made these tasty, flaky meat rolls on special occasions, and when she did, I couldn't wait for my first mouthful. They remind me of a Greek version of burritos, but the béchamel and cheese sauce (Mornay) adds sophistication.

The traditional method for rolling the phyllo is tedious and time-consuming, but thanks to a technique I learned while watching a TV episode of Ina Garten's *Barefoot Contessa*, rolling these takes little time—plus they're fun to make. To borrow an oft-used phrase from the Contessa herself, "Your guests will think you spent hours in the kitchen."

Makes 12 (6-inch) rolls

Meat Mixture

1½ **pounds ground beef or lamb**

1½ **cups shredded Monterey Jack cheese**

½ **cup grated Parmesan cheese**

¼ **cup extra virgin olive oil**

1 **medium onion, finely chopped**

2 **medium cloves garlic, finely chopped**

2 **medium stalks celery, finely chopped**

½ **cup loosely packed flat-leaf (Italian) parsley, finely chopped**

3 **large white button mushrooms, stems removed, rinsed and finely chopped**

2 **tablespoons dry white wine, such as Chardonnay**

Salt and freshly ground black pepper

¾ **teaspoon cinnamon**

3 **eggs, lightly beaten**

Phyllo

8 **sheets phyllo, #4 (fine)**

½ **cup (1 stick) butter, melted**

Parchment paper

<u>Béchamel and Cheese Sauce</u> (Mornay)

1 ¼ cups regular or 2% fat milk, plus a little extra on hand if needed

3 tablespoons butter

2 tablespoons all-purpose flour

½ teaspoon salt

⅓ cup shredded Monterey Jack cheese

Read Appendix A, *Being At Ease with Phyllo* (see page 321).

For the Meat: Brown meat in a large (5-quart) saucepan on medium-high heat; drain fat. Transfer meat to a plate and set aside near the stove along with the Monterey Jack and Parmesan cheeses. Wipe pot for next use.

Pour olive oil into the same pot and add onion and garlic. Cook on medium heat for 2-3 minutes, or until soft, stirring occasionally. Add celery, parsley, mushrooms, wine, 1 teaspoon salt, and dash pepper. Stir to combine well and cook on medium heat for 5 minutes, stirring occasionally.

Add browned meat, ¾ teaspoon salt, dash pepper, and cinnamon; stir to combine well.

Add Monterey Jack and Parmesan cheeses to meat mixture and stir until melted and combined well. Remove pot from burner and tilt pot to see if any liquid runs to the bottom. If so, drain with paper towels.

With the pot off the burner, add lightly beaten eggs and stir until combined well. Cook over low heat about 5 minutes, stirring continuously, until the eggs set and are absorbed into the mixture. Adjust to taste. Pour into a bowl and refrigerate for at least one hour.

For the Phyllo: Preheat oven to 325 degrees. Line 1 to 2 large (15 x 10 x 1-inch) baking sheets with parchment paper; set aside.

After the meat mixture has refrigerated for at least one hour, place the bowl containing the mixture near the melted butter and phyllo. Place one sheet of phyllo horizontally (with the long side facing you) on a large cutting board or work surface and brush lightly, but completely, with the melted butter. Layer a second sheet over the first one and brush again.

Place heaping tablespoons of the meat mixture along the lower horizontal edge starting from 1 inch away from the bottom. With both hands, roll the phyllo to the end. Seal the edge by brushing with butter. Transfer the roll to the prepared baking sheet and score it diagonally into thirds. Brush the top and sides of the roll with butter. Repeat this process 3 more times with the remainder of the meat and phyllo. Place in preheated oven and bake for 25 minutes, or until phyllo is lightly golden. *(Note: These freeze well. If you wish to freeze, cover the pan(s) of uncooked rolls with aluminum foil and place in freezer. When ready to use, preheat oven to same temperature, remove foil, and cook about 30 minutes.)*

For the Béchamel and Cheese Sauce: Heat milk in a small pot until just below the boiling point; set aside. Melt butter in a small, heavy-bottomed saucepan over medium heat. When melted, add flour and stir with a whisk to blend until smooth. Gradually add hot milk, stirring continuously, until mixture is smooth. Add salt and cheese and stir until melted and velvety. *(Note: If sauce gets too thick, add dash milk to loosen.)* Cut through the rolls where scored and transfer to a serving plate. Spoon béchamel sauce over rolls; serve hot.

Pastitsio

Pastitisio is not only beloved in Greece, but in our home as well. It's very similar to lasagna with its layers of pasta and beef, but in this case finishes with a layer of béchamel and cheese (Mornay) sauce. Traditionally, pastitsio is made with hollow, tube-shaped pasta, such as candele, bucatini, or long ziti, but spaghetti will do just fine.

From the "ele's," "ini's," "iti's," and "etti's," you may be wondering if this dish is more Italian than Greek—with good reason. For nearly four hundred years, Greece's northwest region, the Ionian Islands—located only a few miles from the Italian coast—was under Venetian rule. Their influence can still be seen in the Greek arts today, namely in its architecture and cuisine.

A final word: Some Greek dishes are known for the number of pots, pans, and bowls used to prepare them—plus all the cleaning required after. Pastitsio is one of them! But don't let that be a hindrance—this casserole-style meal is worth your time, effort, and dishpan hands.

Serves 12

Meat

1⅓ pounds ground beef

¼ cup extra virgin olive oil

1 medium onion

2 medium cloves garlic

Salt and freshly ground pepper

1 (15-ounce) can tomato sauce

2 tablespoons tomato paste

¼ cup dry white wine, such as Chardonnay

2 tablespoons water

1½ teaspoons sugar

½ teaspoon oregano

½ teaspoon ground cinnamon

1 bay leaf

Pasta
1 ½ pounds dry spaghetti

1 tablespoon butter

1 tablespoon extra virgin olive oil

3 teaspoons salt

¾ cup grated Parmesan cheese

Béchamel and Cheese Sauce (Mornay)
1 ½ quarts (6 cups) whole or 2% low-fat milk, plus a little extra if needed

¾ cup (1 ½ sticks) butter

¾ cups all-purpose flour

2 teaspoons salt

1 ½ cups grated Parmesan cheese

6 eggs

For the Meat: Pour ¼ cup olive oil into a large (5-quart) saucepan. Add onion, garlic, ½ teaspoon salt, and dash pepper. Cook on medium heat for 2-3 minutes, or until soft, stirring occasionally. Break up meat into small pieces and add to onion mixture. Brown meat; drain fat.

Add tomato sauce, tomato paste, wine, and water; stir until combined well. Bring mixture to a boil. Reduce to medium-low heat. Add sugar, ¾ teaspoon salt, dash pepper, oregano, cinnamon, and bay leaf; stir until combined well. Cook for 20 minutes, partially covered, until the sauce has thickened. Adjust to taste. Discard bay leaf; set meat sauce aside.

Grease a large (15 x 10 x 2-inch) baking pan; set aside.

For the Pasta: Fill a large (5-quart) saucepan two-thirds full with water and bring to a boil. In bunches, break dry spaghetti in half and place in boiling water. Cook al dente, or according to package directions. Drain well and return to pot. Add 1 tablespoon butter, 1 tablespoon olive oil, and 3 teaspoons salt; stir until combined well.

To Assemble: Place half the cooked spaghetti in the prepared pan and arrange in an even layer. Add half the cheese, distributing evenly. Add the meat mixture over the pasta and smooth evenly. Add the remaining spaghetti, distributing evenly. Add the remaining cheese; set aside.

For the Béchamel and Cheese Sauce: Set aside a large bowl for later use. Pour milk into a saucepan and cook on medium heat until just before it starts to boil; remove from heat and set aside.

Measure 1½ cups Parmesan cheese and place near the stove along with 2 teaspoons salt.

Melt ¾ cup butter in a large (5-quart) saucepan on medium heat. Gradually add flour, stirring continuously with a whisk, until smooth and mixture starts to bubble. Add hot milk and stir continuously until mixture is smooth and thick. *(Note: If the mixture becomes too thick, reduce heat and add a little more milk. Likewise, if it becomes too runny, increase heat until it thickens.)* Add 1½ teaspoons salt and cheese and stir until melted and smooth. Remove pot from burner. Pour mixture into the large bowl and cool for 20 minutes, stirring occasionally to release steam.

Preheat oven to 350 degrees 10 minutes before the milk mixture has cooled.

After the milk mixture has cooled for 20 minutes, beat eggs in a medium bowl for 30 seconds. Fold* eggs into milk mixture until smooth. Pour evenly over the spaghetti. Place pan in preheated oven and bake for 25 minutes. Reduce heat to 325 degrees and bake for another 25-30 minutes, or until golden brown or a toothpick inserted in the center comes out clean. Cool for at least 20 to 30 minutes for the top layer to set. Cut into pieces; serve hot.
(*Note: To fold in the eggs, "cut" the mixture in half vertically with a spatula, bring the spatula down and across the bottom of the bowl, and then turn it over into the mixture. Keep repeating until you've achieved an even blend.)

Pam's Chili

Cozy (adj.): snug, comfortable, and warm.[7]

This word conjures memories from one particular Gourmet Club dinner.

The theme was Ye Olde English Christmas. When the hostess welcomed my date and me inside her apartment, I thought I had just entered a small library inside a limestone cottage in the Cotswolds—an intimate air was palpable. To illustrate, aside from the colored lights from her Christmas tree, only flickering candles lit a dark living room adorned with books, family photos, and interesting artifacts. And nearby, two round dining tables—one wearing a deep red cloth and the other a forest green—were set with bone china edged in roses while antique silver nestled close by. Were we really in an old village in rural Chedworth?

After the other Club members and their dates arrived, we toasted with a hearty "Hear, Hear!" over a glass of hot mulled wine to kick off the evening before enjoying the Liver Paté on Toasted Triangles, and Cheese Logs with Waverly crackers that someone brought for appetizers. Amidst lively cheer and chatter, we eventually took our seats for dinner not knowing what to expect next. Then, lo and behold! The hostess foxtrotted from the kitchen wielding a large pewter platter of Rice-Stuffed Roasted Duck Garnished with Fresh Herbs. We were dazzled by the sight as the mood quickly transformed from merry to magical.

Later on, I was a little sorry when the tasty Prune Pudding with Hard Sauce and Tom and Jerry cordials were served. I knew our evening (and "travel") was coming to a close. But all was not lost. After expressing our gratitude at the door, we uttered, "Well, best be off, cheerio!" and confessed feeling more akin to our friends across the pond.

*

For me, a steaming bowl of chili arouses those same warm emotions as that Ye Olde English Christmas dinner from years ago. And to vouch for its popularity, there are as many versions of this American favorite as there are people who love it. Here's mine—it's tomatoey, meaty, and succulent.

For this recipe I use the mild Anaheim chile, but if your heat threshold leans more toward "burn," use the jalapeño or serrano instead. For a casual lunch or dinner, serve it with Fresh Mixed Green Salad and Cornbread (see pages 97 and 134). I promise you won't be disappointed.

Serves 8

2 pounds ground beef

⅓ pound ground pork

1 pound dried kidney beans

3 mild Anaheim chiles

⅓ cup extra virgin olive oil

1 medium onion, finely chopped

3-4 cloves garlic, finely chopped

Salt and freshly ground black pepper

1 (16-ounce) can whole, peeled tomatoes, including juices

3 (11.5-ounce) cans tomato juice

½ cup white wine

1½ tablespoons extra virgin olive oil

1 tablespoon plus 1 teaspoon chili powder

1½ teaspoons sugar

<u>Toppings</u> (optional)

Cheddar cheese (sharp), grated

Onion, finely chopped

Sour cream

Advance Preparation: Place beans in a large bowl and cover with water. Soak overnight; drain in a colander.

Place the drained beans in a large (5-quart) saucepan and cover with water. Bring to a boil and cook for 40 minutes, or until tender, adding water as needed. Drain and set aside. Wipe down the pot for next use.

Core chiles and cut in half lengthwise. Remove membranes and seeds; rinse and pat dry with paper towels. Slice lengthwise into quarters then into eighths. In bunches, gather strips and dice crosswise; set aside.

Pour ⅓ cup olive oil into the same pot. Add onion and garlic and cook on medium heat for 2-3 minutes, or until soft, stirring occasionally. Break up ground beef and pork into small pieces and add to onion mixture. Add 1 teaspoon salt and dash pepper and cook until meat is browned, stirring occasionally; drain fat. Set aside from burner.

Process whole, peeled tomatoes in a food processor for about 10 seconds and add to meat mixture; stir until combined well.

Add cooked kidney beans, tomato juice, diced chiles, wine, 1½ tablespoons olive oil, chili powder, 2½ teaspoons salt, ½ teaspoon ground pepper, and sugar; stir until combined well. Return to burner and bring to a boil. Reduce heat to medium low and cook for 1 hour, partially covered, stirring occasionally. Adjust to taste; serve hot. Place toppings in small bowls, if desired, and serve alongside chili.

Scrumptious Lasagna

Though Italian in origin, lasagna is so beloved America has adopted it as its own. My mother's version of this classic dish is simply luscious.

Serves 12

Meat Sauce

2½ **pounds ground beef**

⅓ **cup extra virgin olive oil,
    plus a little extra on hand**

1 **large onion, finely chopped**

6 **cloves garlic, finely chopped**

**Salt and freshly ground
    black pepper**

3 **(6-ounce) cans tomato paste**

3 **cups water**

2 **(15-ounce) cans tomato sauce**

½ **cup dry white wine, such as
    Chardonnay**

2 **tablespoons sugar**

2 **bay leaves**

1½ **teaspoons cinnamon**

2 **teaspoons oregano**

Pasta

1-**pound package dry lasagna**

1 **tablespoon salt**

Aluminum foil

Egg and Cheese Filling

2 **(8-ounce) containers fresh,
    ovaline (egg-size) mozzarella
    cheese balls packed in water**

6 **eggs**

1 **(15-ounce) container ricotta
    cheese**

1 **cup grated Parmesan cheese**

¾ **cup loosely packed flat-leaf
    (Italian) parsley, finely chopped**

½ **teaspoons salt**

¼ **cup grated Parmesan cheese,
    reserved for the topping**

For the Meat Sauce: Pour ⅓ cup olive oil into a large (5-quart) saucepan. Add onion, garlic, ½ teaspoon salt, and dash pepper and cook on medium heat 2-3 minutes, or until soft, stirring occasionally. Break up meat into small pieces and add to onion mixture. Add 1 teaspoon salt and dash pepper; stir to combine well. Cook until meat is browned; drain fat. Remove from heat.

Place tomato paste into a medium bowl and add water. Stir with a whisk until smooth. Place meat mixture back over heat and add tomato paste mixture, tomato sauce, wine, sugar, bay leaves, cinnamon, and oregano. Swirl in a little bit of olive oil.

Stir to combine well and bring to a boil. Reduce heat to medium-low and cook for 30-40 minutes, partially covered, stirring occasionally. Discard bay leaves. Reserve 2 cups meat sauce and set aside.

For the Pasta: Fill a large stockpot three-quarters full of water and bring to a boil. Add 1 tablespoon salt. Add lasagna strips one at a time and cook for 10 minutes, or according to package directions; drain in a colander. Separate strips and place them on a sheet of aluminum foil so they don't stick together.

For the Egg and Cheese Filling: Drain mozzarella balls in a colander and cut into thin slices; set aside on a plate.

Place the eggs in a medium mixing bowl and beat with a portable electric mixer about 25 seconds. Add ricotta cheese, 1 cup Parmesan cheese, parsley, and ½ teaspoon salt. Blend together on low speed to combine well; set aside.

To Assemble: Preheat oven to 350 degrees.

Spread a light layer of meat sauce all around the bottom of a large (15½ x 10½ x 2¼-inch) baking pan. Arrange one layer of lasagna strips by slightly overlapping the edges. Add half of the egg and cheese filling, spreading evenly. Add half of the mozzarella slices, distributing evenly. Add half of the meat sauce, spreading evenly. Repeat, starting with another layer of lasagna strips and so on until the strips are all used. For the topmost layer, add the reserved meat sauce, spreading evenly.

Place in preheated oven and cook for 15 minutes. After 15 minutes, cover the pan tightly with aluminum foil and cook for another 20 minutes. Remove from oven and let stand, uncovered, for 15 minutes. Add reserved Parmesan cheese; serve hot.

Tomato and Meat Sauce for Spaghetti

My mother's spaghetti sauce recipe is meaty, delicious, and has been known to produce those familiar, yet impolite, slurping sounds. Invariably, it's the first thing our youngest son asks for when he arrives home from college. As a matter of fact, I still cherish a memory of him as a toddler devouring Mom's tomato and meat sauce with spaghetti from his Spot the Dog melamine bowl. Even I can't think of a more satisfying meal, especially when served with Fresh Mixed Green Salad and Authentic Sourdough Garlic Bread (see pages 97 and 141). Good honest food never disappoints.

I usually make enough for leftovers, and think it tastes better the second or third night after the flavors have had time to blend. Plus, it freezes beautifully—a welcome convenience for those nights you don't feel like cooking. After a few bites, I wouldn't be surprised if even you shout "Mamma Mia"!

Serves 10

1 ½ pounds lean ground beef

½ pound ground pork

¼ cup extra virgin olive oil

1 medium onion, finely chopped

**3 medium cloves garlic,
finely chopped**

½ pound white button mushrooms

**¾ cup loosely packed flat-leaf
(Italian) parsley, finely chopped**

**¾ cup dry white wine, such as
Chardonnay**

**Salt and freshly ground
black pepper**

1 (6-ounce) can tomato paste

1 cup water

1 (28-ounce) can plum tomatoes

2 bay leaves

1 ½ teaspoons dried oregano

1 ½ teaspoons sugar

1 teaspoon ground cinnamon

½ cup water, plus extra as needed

Dry, uncooked spaghetti as needed

Freshly grated Parmesan cheese

Break up meat into small pieces and place in a large (5-quart) saucepan. Cook on medium-high heat until browned, stirring occasionally; drain fat. Transfer meat to a plate or bowl; set aside. Wipe pot clean with a paper towel for next use.

Trim stems from mushrooms; discard stems. Scrub mushroom caps under cold water to remove dirt particles; pat dry with paper towels. Slice into halves or thirds, depending on size; set aside on a plate.

Place olive oil, onion, and garlic into cleaned pot and cook on medium heat for 2-3 minutes or until soft, stirring occasionally. Add mushrooms, parsley, wine, 1 teaspoon salt, and dash pepper; stir until combined well. Cook for 5 minutes. Meanwhile, place canned tomatoes in a food processor and process for 8-10 seconds; set aside.

After the mixture has cooked 5 minutes, add tomato paste and 1 cup water. Incorporate the paste into the mixture with the back of a wooden spoon, and stir until combined well. Add processed tomatoes and browned meat; stir until combined.

Add bay leaves, oregano, sugar, 1½ teaspoons salt, dash pepper, cinnamon, and ½ cup water; stir until combined well. Bring mixture to a boil. Reduce heat to medium-low and cook, partially covered, for 1 hour. *(Note: The consistency should be loose enough to stir comfortably, but not runny. If the mixture is too thick, add water ½ cup at a time until you achieve desired consistency.)* Adjust to taste.

Cook spaghetti, using the amount desired, according to package directions; drain. Drizzle with olive oil and add salt to taste. Ladle sauce over cooked spaghetti and add freshly grated Parmesan cheese, if desired. Serve hot.

Prized Family Meatloaf

When my parents bought me a lunch card for the cafeteria in second grade, I was introduced to a different sort of cuisine than I had been accustomed—American Traditional. There, for the first time, I ate Sloppy Joes, meatloaf and mashed potatoes, fried chicken and biscuits, plus desserts like apple crisp and cherry cobbler. Needless to say, I loved every bite! Later on, I realized these American dishes were a seamless counterpart to the humble, authentic fare of Greek home cooking.

When it comes to meat dishes, I don't know of any other that spells Americana more than meatloaf. Although numerous recipes exist, I love this one. After noticing it in a popular magazine, I just knew I had to try it, and this simplified rendition has been in my recipe collection ever since. (By the way, the original recipe comes from the Smith family—you can't get any more Anglo-Saxon than that!) The secret to its wonderful flavor is the ketchup sauce—you'll know what I mean when you try it. (Adapted with permission; *Better Homes & Gardens,* May 2002.)

Serves 8

Ketchup Sauce

¾ **cup ketchup**

2 **tablespoons Worcestershire sauce**

2 **tablespoons light brown sugar**

2 **teaspoons regular or low-sodium soy sauce**

1½ **teaspoons dry mustard**

Meat Mixture

¾ **cup ground beef**

½ **pound ground pork**

¼ **pound ground veal**

½ **medium onion, grated or finely chopped**

2 **medium cloves garlic, finely chopped**

¼ **cup loosely packed flat-leaf Italian) parsley, finely chopped**

2 **eggs**

½ **cup dried breadcrumbs**

1 **tablespoon regular or 2% low-fat milk**

1½ **teaspoons salt**

Dash freshly ground black pepper

Preheat oven to 400 degrees.

For the Ketchup Sauce: Pour ketchup, Worcestershire sauce, brown sugar, soy sauce, and dry mustard in a medium bowl. Stir with a whisk until combined well. Set aside.

For the Meat Mixture: Place the ground beef, pork, and veal in medium bowl. Add onion, garlic, parsley, eggs, breadcrumbs, milk, salt, and pepper. Add one-third cup of the ketchup sauce. Mix by hand until combined well.

Transfer mixture to a 9 x 5 x 3-inch nonstick (preferred) loaf pan and form into a loaf shape. Pour another third of the ketchup mixture over meat, distributing evenly. Place in preheated oven and cook for 15 minutes. Reduce to 350 degrees and cook for another 45-50 minutes. Let cool for 10 minutes. Warm the remaining ketchup mixture in a small pot or microwave and serve alongside each serving.

Sweet Things

Butter Cookies
Kourambiethes

My happiest childhood memories were the weekends I spent with my maternal grand-parents at their apartment in San Francisco. My *yiayia* (grandmother) barely spoke English, and I a scant Greek, but we seemed to communicate without any problem. I especially looked forward to our outings together. We shopped at I. Magnin on Geary Street and ate lunch next door at Blum's where we would order a Monte Cristo or Monte Carlo (plus a chocolate shake for me). Afterward, we walked across the street to Union Square to feed the pigeons with dry scraps of bread from dinner the night before. Other days, we ventured to Sausalito and ate homemade sandwiches on the large boulders overlooking the bay, then strolled along the Bridgeway with our Japanese-style paper parasols. Even those times *yiayia* and I snuggled together on her living room sofa and watched *Lassie* or *I Love Lucy* were special. At bedtime, she told scary stories about forest people.

As for my *papou* (grandfather), he was determined I learn to speak Greek. When he arrived home from work, *papou* would remove his collar and black jacket and put on his silk smoking jacket and backless leather slippers. Then he would seat me on his knee, pull out a Greek grammar book, and pay *me* ten cents a page to learn the pronunciation of those strange curlicue characters. But I didn't mind the lesson. When it was over, *papou* bounced me on his knee and sang a rhyming song, *"Po po, po, na ta haro"* ("Oh, oh, my, I love her").

When he wasn't around, I'd sneak into his den and play office. I loved perching myself in front of his black Underwood typewriter, rolling in a sheet of paper, yanking the carriage back, and pressing the metal keys with all my might. My grandparents were fun, and when my mother came to pick me up on Sunday nights, I cried.

My mother's recipe for butter cookies conjures those same warm and joyful memories from my childhood. Adorned by a thick, pristine coat of powdered sugar, they're as pretty as a bride on her wedding day. It's no wonder butter cookies are traditionally made for special occasions, such as baptisms, weddings, or name days (feast days of the year that honor the saint associated with one's Christian name). But with so much deliciousness, why wait for a celebration to enjoy them?

The secret to their soft, velvety, melt-in-your-mouth crumb is the time spent whipping the butter—fifteen minutes for this recipe. Let's just say eating one is like getting a big bear hug.

Makes 30 cookies

Cookie Dough
2 cups plus 2 tablespoons all-purpose flour, sifted

½ pound (2 sticks) unsalted butter, softened

½ cup granulated sugar

1 egg yolk

2 tablespoons plus 2 teaspoons whiskey

Topping

1 cup confectioners (powdered) sugar

1 package paper baking cups

For the Cookie Dough: Place the softened butter in a large bowl and beat for 15 minutes, or until the color is off-white and has the consistency of mayonnaise, stopping once or twice to scrape down sides of bowl. Gradually add granulated sugar and beat for 2 minutes, or until the mixture is fluffy, stopping once to scrape. Add the egg yolk and whiskey and beat until combined well.

Gradually add sifted flour and mix until combined, stopping once or twice to scrape.

Preheat oven to 325 degrees. Set aside 2 ungreased (15 x 10 x 1-inch) baking sheets.

Measure a full tablespoon of dough and form a ball shape by rolling it between the palms of your hand. *(Note: If the dough is too sticky and unworkable, add 1 tablespoon sifted flour and stir with a spatula to combine.)* Transfer to baking sheet and repeat for the remaining dough.

Place baking sheets in preheated oven and bake for 15-18 minutes, or until the underside of the cookie is a light golden color.

For the Topping: Right after the cookies are out of the oven and still hot, sift confectioners sugar on top, forming a generous coat; let cool a few minutes.

With the corner edge of a spatula, take up a little of the surrounding confectioners sugar and place on the bottom of a paper baking cup to coat the underside of each cookie. With the corner edge again, transfer cookie to the paper baking cup. Repeat for the remaining cookies. Serve or store in an airtight container. Will stay fresh up to 2 weeks.

Twist Cookies with Sesame Seeds
Koulourakia

Sometimes when I came home from grade school, I found my mother seated at our laminate kitchen table rolling these cookies on a wooden board. "Can I help?" I would ask. "Sure," my mother replied, while handing me a board and chunk of dough of my own. For some reason, it was here in this modest kitchen—with its deep, rust-colored linoleum underfoot, mustard-colored refrigerator, and orange and yellow floral, vinyl wallpaper—that I felt most secure.

First, I observed my mother handle the dough, and tried to imitate her ways. Then I examined the way she brushed the egg wash and sprinkled sesame seeds over each cookie as if I were studying for a test the following day. Mostly, we formed the dough into twist shapes, but sometimes we made them into circles or S-shapes while singing this song in Greek: "Mold them with your little hands, put them in the oven, and the whole house will smell good." I didn't know it then, but these cozy transactions were the seeds of a lifelong passion to cook.

Puffy and light, this simple cookie is perfect with a cup of coffee or tea. Traditionally, they're made at Easter, but they're so tasty, why wait until then?

Makes about 4 dozen

Parchment paper

Dough

4¼ cups all-purpose flour

2 teaspoons baking powder

½ teaspoon baking soda

1 teaspoon ground cinnamon

¾ cup (1½ sticks) unsalted butter, softened

¼ cup vegetable oil

1¼ cups sugar

3 eggs

3 tablespoons half-and-half or milk

1 teaspoon vanilla extract

Egg Wash

1 egg yolk

2 teaspoons milk

1 teaspoon water

Topping

2 tablespoons sesame seeds (optional)

For the Dough: Line 3 (15 x 10 x 1-inch) baking sheets with parchment paper; set aside.

Sift flour, baking powder, baking soda, and cinnamon together in a bowl; set aside.

Place softened butter in a large mixing bowl and beat on high speed 2-3 minutes. Add oil and mix until combined well, stopping once to scrape down the sides of the bowl.

Gradually add sugar and beat for 2-3 minutes until pale yellow and fluffy, stopping once to scrape.

Add eggs, one at a time, beating well after each addition, stopping once to scrape.

Add half-and-half and vanilla extract. Mix until combined well.

Gradually add flour mixture until combined well, stopping once or twice to scrape. Cover with plastic wrap and refrigerate for 1 hour.

Preheat oven to 325 degrees. Scoop out a full tablespoon of dough and roll into a ball between the palms of your hands. Place ball on a wooden board and roll into a 6-inch-long rope. Then, form rope into a sideways U-shape. Lift rope with both hands and twist 3 times; place on prepared baking sheet. Repeat with remaining dough, placing each cookie about 1 inch apart.

For the Egg Wash: Place egg yolk in a small bowl and add milk and water. Beat with a fork until combined well. Dip the tips of a pastry brush into the egg wash and brush the top of each cookie. Add sesame seeds and place in preheated oven. Cook for 25 minutes, or until the color is light golden; cool. Store in an airtight container. Will stay fresh for up to 3 weeks.

Honey-Dipped Spice Cookies
Melomakarona

Besides being a dedicated wife and mother, my paternal grandmother co-founded a Greek Ladies' Society called *Prodos* (Progress) whose primary aim was to preserve the Greek language and culture in San Francisco. I know little about this worthwhile organization, except for the tea parties these ladies often gave in honor of someone or some special event.

By all accounts, these formal and elegant afternoon occasions were worthy of Emily Post. Here, the well-dressed hostess would gather all her "bests"—bone china, linen napkins and tablecloths, and lace doilies—and display them with pride. But the most treasured possession of this paraphernalia was her silver tea set. Whether simple or ornate, this gleaming apparatus was a bustling post for serving hot coffee and tea, cream, and lumps of sugar. (With all their loveliness, however, when not in use these tea sets were barely recognizable. Greek women, it seems, have a predilection for wrapping these heirlooms in layers of heavy, clear plastic to minimize tarnishing.)

As for the food, these affairs were no place for slurping spaghettis or lofty lasagnas. Instead, they sported dainty edibles such as triangle-shaped tea sandwiches or deviled eggs placed on tiered cake stands. Really, any finger food that minimized spill on silk or chiffon was acceptable. However, dessert invited a little more risk. How else were those crumbly, syrupy Greek sweets so neatly tucked in paper baking cups to be savored without making a real go of it?

But despite these social affairs, I think Grandma felt most comfortable at home in her kitchen. There she could relax, visit with family, talk with her friends on the telephone, and peruse her black leather book that contained all her handwritten recipes. They were the soul of her proud Greek heritage.

While flipping through this black leather book in her kitchen one afternoon, I arrived at her formula for *Melomakarona* (traditional oblong-shaped, honey-dipped cookies). These delicious cookies were my father's favorite, and are mine, too. So, I copied her formula on a piece of scratch paper.

Back at home, I tweaked a little here, shuffled a little there, and experimented with a fitting equivalent to a "jigger of whiskey," but remained steadfast to Grandma's test for doneness. On this subject she wrote, "Make sure the dough is not tough, but soft, as you want the cookies to melt in your mouth." Grandma, I think you'd be pleased.

Makes 25 cookies

<u>**Walnuts**</u>

⅓ cup shelled walnuts

<u>**Syrup**</u>

1½ cups water

¾ cup sugar

¾ cup clover honey

1 cinnamon stick

2 strips orange peel

2-3 whole cloves

<u>**Cookie Dough**</u>

¼ cup orange juice

¼ teaspoon baking soda

3 cups all-purpose flour

1¼ teaspoon baking powder

⅛ teaspoon salt

½ teaspoon ground cinnamon,
  plus extra for topping

¼ teaspoon ground cloves

½ cup butter (1 stick), softened

¾ cup canola oil

¼ cup plus 1 tablespoon sugar

1 egg

2 tablespoons whiskey

Paper baking cups

For the Walnuts: Preheat oven to 325 degrees. Place shelled walnuts on a large (15 x 10 x 1-inch) baking sheet and toast in preheated oven for 10-12 minutes; cool. Chop finely; set aside.

For the Syrup: Place the water, sugar, honey, cinnamon stick, orange strips, and cloves in a medium (3-quart) saucepan. Bring to a boil and stir until combined well. Reduce heat to low and cook for 15-20 minutes without stirring. Remove from burner; set aside.

For the Cookie Dough: Add baking soda to orange juice and stir with a fork until uniform; set aside.

Sift together flour, baking powder, salt, ½ teaspoon cinnamon, and cloves in a medium bowl; set aside.

Place softened butter in a large mixing bowl and beat for 1-2 minutes. Gradually stir in the oil, stopping once to scrape down the sides of the bowl with a spatula.

One at a time, add the sugar, egg, orange juice mixture, and whiskey, blending after each addition.

Add sifted flour mixture a little at a time, blending after each addition until the flour disappears. Stop once or twice to scrape. *(Note: The dough should feel soft and moist, yet come away from the sides of the bowl. If not, add 1 or 2 tablespoons sifted flour.)*

Preheat oven to 325 degrees. Set aside 2 (15 x 10 x 1-inch) ungreased baking sheets.

To form the cookies, measure 1½ heaping tablespoons of dough and roll into a ball with your palms. Gently squeeze the ball between your palms then mold into an oblong shape like an egg. Place on pan and *lightly press* with the tines of a fork without flattening it. Repeat for the remaining dough. Place pan in preheated oven and bake for 30 minutes.

Meanwhile, place a sheet of waxed or parchment paper under a wire cooling rack near the syrup. Remove cinnamon stick, peel, and cloves from the syrup; discard.

After the cookies have baked for 30 minutes and are still hot, submerge one or two at a time in the syrup until coated. With a slotted spoon, transfer cookies to the wire rack. Repeat for the remaining cookies. Sprinkle with walnuts and cinnamon. Transfer to paper baking cups. Serve, or store in airtight container.

Crazy Lemon Cake

If you're a lemon aficionado like me, you'll understand why this is called crazy. One evening, my girlfriend Marcia Signori served this moist cake at a dinner party, and it just titillated my palate. By the way, I hope you won't be discouraged by the prepared cake mix. After all, what's wrong with a little help in the kitchen?

Serves 8

Cake Batter

1 (15-ounce) box lemon-cake mix, super moist preferred

1 (3-ounce) package lemon gelatin

4 eggs

¾ cup vegetable oil

¾ cup water

Glaze

½ cup confectioners (powdered) sugar

3 tablespoons lemon juice

Topping

2-3 tablespoons confectioners (powdered) sugar

For the Batter: Preheat oven to 350 degrees. Grease a nonstick fluted or plain tube pan; set aside.

Place cake mix, gelatin, eggs, vegetable oil, and water in a large bowl and mix with a handheld electric beater for 2 minutes, stirring once to scrape down the sides. Pour into prepared pan and place in preheated oven. Cook for 35 to 40 minutes, or until a toothpick inserted in the center comes out clean.

For the Glaze: Sift ½ cup confectioners sugar in a medium bowl. Add lemon juice and stir with a whisk or fork until dissolved; set aside.

After the cake is done and still in the pan, poke deep holes with a sharp knife or ice pick, and spoon inside half of the glaze. Loosen the edges of the pan with a knife and invert the cake onto a 10½-inch plate. Repeat poking holes on the top and spoon inside the remainder of the glaze. Let stand for at least 1 hour to cool completely.

For the Topping: Dust (or sift) 2-3 tablespoons confectioners sugar over cake. Cut in slices and serve.

Walnut Cake with Syrup
Karidopita Horis Siropi

My mother's oldest sister Chrys enjoyed indulging herself with the pleasures in life—pretty clothes, good food, dance, and nice husbands. She also loved to cook, and I'm grateful her recipe for Walnut Cake with Syrup came my way. It's simply scrumptious, especially teamed with a steaming cup of tea on a cool autumn day when all you want to do is curl up on the sofa with a knitted throw. As a matter of fact, just thinking about its moist crumb, rugged texture, and sweet, rich flavor can transform the moment from brisk to bliss.

Makes 24 pieces

Walnuts

1 ½ cups shelled walnut halves

Syrup

¾ cup water

¾ cup sugar

¾ cup clover honey

1 teaspoon lemon juice

1 cinnamon stick

Batter

2 cups pancake mix

1 cup sugar

1½ teaspoons baking powder

1 teaspoon ground cinnamon

½ teaspoon ground cloves

⅛ teaspoon salt

1 cup regular or 2% low-fat milk

1 cup vegetable oil

4 eggs, lightly beaten

For the Walnuts: Preheat oven to 325 degrees. Place walnuts on a large (15 x 10 x 1-inch) baking sheet and arrange in a single layer. Toast in preheated oven for 10-12 minutes; cool for 5 minutes. Chop walnuts coarsely; set aside.

For the Syrup: Place water, sugar, honey, lemon juice, and cinnamon stick in a small, heavy-bottomed saucepan. Bring to a boil while stirring until the sugar is dissolved and ingredients are combined well. Reduce to low heat and cook another 20 minutes without stirring; set aside.

For the Batter: Preheat oven to 325 degrees. Grease and lightly flour a medium (13 x 9 x 2-inch) baking pan; set aside.

Place the pancake mix, sugar, baking powder, ground cinnamon, ground cloves, and salt in a large mixing bowl. Add the milk, oil, and eggs all at once and mix with a handheld electric beater until the ingredients are combined well. *(Note: Don't worry about clumps—they magically disappear during cooking.)* Add chopped nuts and stir with a spatula. Pour batter in prepared baking pan and place in preheated oven. Bake for 30-35 minutes, or until a toothpick inserted in the center comes out clean. Cool for 10 minutes.

After the cake has cooled for 10 minutes and is still in the pan, cut it diagonally into 2-inch widths starting from the center. Repeat in the opposite direction to form diamond shapes. Discard the cinnamon stick from the syrup. Spoon the syrup into all the cut edges including around the perimeter, and let stand about 30 minutes for the syrup to soak. Serve warm.

Fresh Peach Cobbler

I don't know why, but fresh fruit just tastes better in Greece. As a matter of fact, you could even say that it achieves VIP status. Home cooks and restaurant owners alike take special care in selecting only the best for their tables—with good reason. Fresh fruit occupies a preeminent role not only as a healthy afternoon snack, but as dessert, too. Besides, it offers cool, juicy goodness in the blazing Mediterranean heat—at least, it did for me those summers I lived in Athens. And oh, did it fancy my palate.

Take the succulent *karpouzi* (watermelon), for instance. I don't know of another food more effective in hosing the sear and sweat than this fire-engine-red one. As for the luscious *verikoka* (apricots), they were plump, meaty, and just the right balance of sugar and tart. And the *rodakina* (peaches)? How they dripped with juice as sweet as honey! Even watching my *papou* (grandfather) peeling and slicing a peach or an apple was a marvel. This happened whenever I joined him for his afternoon snack on the shady veranda.

First, he would clutch the round fruit in his left hand—like a lefty getting ready for a windup—while holding a paring knife in his right. Then he would remove the peel in neat rows by working around the fruit crosswise. Finally, he sliced it lengthwise eating one slice at a time. What an artful technique, I thought. Much better than the stuff-the-whole-thing-in-your-mouth approach I was accustomed to back home.

It was on that same veranda I ate my first fig. One afternoon *papou* had a bundle of them resting on his lap. After he peeled off its purplish-black skin, he offered me one, and I savored its sweet flavor and squishy, nutty texture so much that I asked for more. Suffice to say that in Greece, fresh fruit rules.

That's not to say summer fruit doesn't achieve celebrity status here at home. It does. And when it comes to fruity desserts, nothing spells the season quite like Fresh Peach Cobbler. However, you don't have to finesse peeling the peaches like my *papou*. I know the result will be just as tasty.

For this recipe, I clipped the original version from a magazine, but it has morphed so much over the years that it bears no resemblance to the original. I kept aiming for tender, cooked peaches and a generous, sweet-flavored biscuit crust with some kick, but got so discouraged with having to go back to the drawing board again and again I was ready to wave the white flag. However, after doing a little more research—and thinking I might be getting closer to the desired result—I decided to give the recipe one last try, and…success!

If ever you find yourself in a similar situation, don't give up. The sweet reward often lies just before the surrender. "And let us not grow weary in well doing: for in due season we shall reap, if we faint not [!]." (Galatians 6:9 KJV)

Serves 6

Filling

3 ½ pounds fresh yellow peaches, peeled and sliced into large bite-size pieces (about 5 ½ cups)

½ cup sugar

1 tablespoon cornstarch

¼ cup water

1 teaspoon lemon zest

Vanilla ice cream (optional)

Biscuit Mixture

1 ¼ cup all-purpose flour

½ cup plus 1 tablespoon sugar

2 teaspoons baking powder

½ teaspoon baking soda

½ teaspoon cinnamon, plus a little extra for topping

¼ teaspoon salt

¼ cup plus 1 tablespoon regular or 2% low-fat milk

5 tablespoons butter, melted

1 ½-2 tablespoons sugar (for topping)

For the Filling: Preheat oven to 375 degrees. Place peeled, sliced peaches in a large bowl.

In a separate bowl, stir together the sugar and cornstarch with a whisk until combined well; add to peaches. Add water and lemon zest and stir with a wooden spoon to combine well. Pour into an ungreased 8 x 8 x 2-inch glass baking dish and place in preheated oven. Cook 25-30 minutes or until juice is thick and bubbly. Meanwhile, prepare the biscuit mixture.

For the Biscuit Mixture: Place the flour, ½ cup plus 1 tablespoon sugar, baking powder, baking soda, ½ teaspoon cinnamon, and salt in a large bowl and stir with a whisk until combined well. Add milk and butter and stir just until combined; set aside.

Maintain oven temperature after the peaches have cooked.

Drop large spoonfuls of the biscuit mixture over the peaches, leaving some space between each spoonful. Add 1 ½-2 tablespoons sugar, distributing evenly. Place back inside oven. Bake for 18-22 minutes, or until a toothpick inserted in various locations comes out clean. Sprinkle with ground cinnamon and cool for 1 hour. Serve warm or at room temperature with a scoop of vanilla ice cream, if desired.

Baklava

Inside a vintage box concealed in the recesses of my mother's kitchen cabinet was a heavy metal contraption. On those occasions she lugged it out, I knew she was about to make baklava. First she would clamp and screw the appliance onto the slide-out cutting board located just beneath our white speckled Formica countertop. Then she would screw the funnel in place before finally attaching the hefty metal crank onto its side. This serious device was a nut grinder, and my mother meant business.

Fortunately, today's versions are small, light, and a cinch to use. My nut grinder is indispensable for the heaps of walnuts needed for this recipe. It also ensures an even texture every time, besides being fun to use. (Alternatively, if you prefer a finer, crumblike granule, you can use a food processor.) And to make the job easier, consider preparing the nuts a day or two in advance—just cover with plastic and refrigerate until you're ready to begin the recipe.

As for the syrup, my mother's formula uses equal parts honey, sugar, and water as the foundation. Then citrus's tang and spice's charisma combine to yield a concoction that's smooth and balanced with delicious, complex flavor.

But after the syrup is poured, don't be in a rush to eat a piece. According to our oldest son, an official baklava enthusiast, the longer it basks in the syrup, the more it soaks, and the better it tastes! Then, after bracing yourself for a spell, go ahead and enjoy a slice with a cup of coffee or tea for a nutritious mid-morning or mid-afternoon snack.

Makes 38 pieces

1 (15 x 1 ½-inch) strip cardboard (to use as a cutting guide)

Wax paper

Tape

Walnut Mixture

6 heaping cups shelled walnuts, about 1 ½ pounds

⅓ cup sugar

1 ½ teaspoons orange zest

1 teaspoon cinnamon

¼ teaspoon ground cloves

Phyllo

Syrup

1 cup clover honey (one 12-ounce bottle)

1 cup sugar

1 cup water

2 strips orange peel

1 strip lemon peel

½ teaspoon lemon juice

4 whole cloves

1 cinnamon stick

2 pounds phyllo,* #4 (fine)

1 cup (2 sticks) unsalted butter

Ground cinnamon

Paper baking cups

(*Note: One box of 12 x 17-inch phyllo typically contains 20-24 sheets. As you'll need a total of 22 sheets for this recipe, I always buy 2 boxes just to be safe. Also, you never know if some sheets will be more difficult to handle, so it's nice to have extras on hand. Consider repackaging/refrigerating the leftover sheets for another occasion.)

Read Appendix A, *Being At Ease with Phyllo* (see page 321).

Wrap wax paper around cardboard strip and tape into place (this strip will serve as your cutting guide later on); set aside.

For the Walnuts: Preheat oven to 325 degrees. Place walnuts on 2 large (15 x 10 x 1-inch) baking sheets and arrange in a single layer. Place sheets in preheated oven and toast for 10 minutes; cool completely.

In a nut grinder, chop walnuts finely and place in a bowl. Add sugar, orange zest, ground cinnamon, and ground cloves; stir to combine well. Separate the walnut mixture into thirds using 3 plates, distributing evenly.

For the Honey: Place the honey, sugar, water, orange peel, lemon peel, lemon juice, whole cloves, and cinnamon stick in a small (1-quart) saucepan; stir to combine well. Cook on medium-high heat until the mixture starts to boil. Reduce heat to low and cook, uncovered, for 20 minutes without stirring; set aside.

To Assemble Walnut Mixture and Phyllo: Melt butter in a small saucepan. Using a pastry brush, grease a medium (15½ x 10½ x 2¼-inch) baking pan with melted butter.

Position oven rack to second from the bottom and preheat to 350 degrees.

Place 1 sheet of phyllo in the prepared pan and brush generously with melted butter. Repeat 6 more times so you have a total of 7 layers to form a bottom "crust," being sure to brush each sheet generously with butter. Add one-third of the walnut mixture, distributing evenly.

Place 1 sheet of phyllo over the walnut mixture and brush generously with melted butter. Repeat with 3 more sheets of phyllo for a total of 4 layers, brushing each sheet generously with butter. Add another third of the walnut mixture, distributing evenly.

Repeat, using the remaining walnut mixture.

Place 1 sheet phyllo over the walnut mixture; brush generously. Repeat 6 more times to form the top "crust," being sure to brush each sheet as well as the topmost sheet generously with butter.

With a sharp knife, trim excess phyllo around the sides of the pan by cutting ¼ inch down from the rim and working the knife all around; discard.

Using the cardboard strip as your guide and starting from the center of the pan, cut the baklava diagonally into 1½-inch widths. *(Tip: Try to avoid having the strip touch the phyllo as the two can stick together.)* Repeat in the opposite direction to form diamond shapes. Wipe cardboard strip clean and save for next use.

Place pan in preheated oven and bake for 40-45 minutes, or until golden brown. Transfer to a cooling rack and let stand for 10 minutes.

Remove citrus peels, cloves, and cinnamon stick from the syrup; discard. Using a large spoon, pour the syrup into all the cut areas and around the perimeter. Sprinkle lightly with ground cinnamon and let stand for at least 2 hours for the syrup to soak in; serve.

To store, cover the pan with aluminum foil and refrigerate, or transfer pieces to individual paper baking cups and place in an airtight container. Stays fresh for up to 2 weeks.

Vanilla Ice Cream with Crème de Menthe

My mother prepared this simple, light dessert often for guests, and played it up by serving it in her finest crystal. It's the perfect ending to a big meal, and I can vouch there's never a drop left over. The best part is no cooking is required.

I love the refreshing flavor of mint and the way it awakens the palate, especially when served with a jigger of libation. When combined with chilled cream—well, let's just say you end up with one splendid swirl.

Serves 4

8 generous-size scoops vanilla ice cream

8 tablespoons (½ cup) crème de menthe liqueur

Whipped cream

Your favorite cookie

Fresh mint leaves (optional)

Set aside 4 dessert glasses.

Place 2 generous scoops ice cream inside one dessert glass. Pour 2 tablespoons crème de menthe over the ice cream and add a dollop whipped cream. Serve with your favorite cookie. Garnish with fresh mint leaves, if desired. Repeat for the remaining dessert glasses and serve.

Custard with Phyllo and Syrup
Galaktoboureko

"I am a *noikokyris* (homemaker)," my mother once declared. Despite all the years she worked outside the home, my mother valued this role foremost, and wore the title proudly. Performing her household tasks in earnest—like the way she starched and ironed cuffs and collars, or worked the Goddard's silver polish until you could barely squint—it suffices to say that in matters relating to hearth and home, my mother had moxie.

But don't get the impression she was a Hazel the Maid type—not that there's anything wrong with that. Rather, my mother was graceful, feminine, and had a svelte figure along with that moxie. Add to that her polite and reserved ways, she was indeed a true lady.

Her knack for things domestic was most evident, however, in the kitchen. Was it how she confidently manipulated a spatula and pastry brush or deftly handled phyllo? Or maybe the way she sprinkled cinnamon and peeled garlic? One thing is certain. All these maneuvers, and more, defined her cooking style long before the word *technique* crept into today's culinary vocabulary.

Perhaps no other recipe embodies my mother's domestic talents more than *Galaktoboureko* (Custard with Phyllo and Syrup). I remember how intently she would stir the milk mixture over the stove with a wooden spoon—her favorite kitchen tool. This was the one time she forbade interruption. "Shhh, I can't talk right now," she would say. Eventually, I came to understand why—the milk mixture comprises this recipe's soul and requires careful tending.

My mother's formula uses all-purpose flour, which yields a lighter, creamier custard than the usual farina. As for the syrup, her concoction produces just the right amount of sweetness and flavor to suit me perfectly.

I have to admit that *Galaktoboureko* is one of my favorite foods. Let's just say when I spoon a little syrup in with each bite my eyes close and I drift to another realm. I wonder—could this be the meaning of "thy will be done on earth as it is in heaven"?

Makes 20 to 24 pieces

<u>Syrup</u>

2 cups sugar

1½ cups water

2½ teaspoons lemon juice

3-4 strips orange peel

4 whole cloves

<u>Custard Filling</u>

2 quarts whole or 2% low-fat milk

⅔ cup plus two tablespoons plus 1 teaspoon all-purpose flour

1 pint heavy whipping cream

1 cup (2 sticks) unsalted butter, softened

½ cup plus 2 tablespoons sugar

1 teaspoon powdered vanilla, or 2 teaspoons vanilla extract

12 eggs

½ cup sugar

<u>Phyllo</u>

2 pounds phyllo

1 ½ cups (3 sticks) unsalted butter

Ground cinnamon

Scissors

Read Appendix A, *Being At Ease with Phyllo* (see page 321).

For the Syrup: Place 2 cups sugar, water, lemon juice, orange peel, and cloves into a small (1½-quart) saucepan. Stir over high heat until the sugar dissolves. Bring to a boil then reduce heat to low. Cook for 15-20 minutes without stirring; set aside.

For the Custard Filling: Measure 3 cups of the milk and pour into a bowl. Add flour and stir with a whisk until smooth and creamy, breaking up small lumps with your fingers. Pour mixture into a large (5-quart) heavy-bottomed saucepan and add remaining milk. Add whipping cream, 1 cup softened butter, ½ cup sugar, and vanilla. On medium-high heat, stir continuously with a wooden spoon for 20-25 minutes until butter melts and the mixture thickens, being careful not to scrape the bottom of the pot. Pour milk mixture into an extra-large mixing bowl; set side for one hour to cool, stirring occasionally to release steam. *(Cleaning Tip: Let pot soak overnight with suds.)*

After the milk mixture has cooled, separate the eggs, placing the whites and yolks into separate bowls. Beat egg whites until stiff. Beat egg yolks, gradually adding ½ cup sugar, until the mixture is thick and pale yellow. Add the yolk mixture to the whites and mix on low speed until combined well.

Add the egg mixture to the cooled milk mixture and mix on low speed until combined well.

To Assemble the Phyllo and Custard Mixture: Preheat oven to 350 degrees. Melt 1½ cups butter in a small saucepan on low heat. Using a pastry brush, grease the bottom and sides of an extra-large (15¾ x 12 x 2¾-inch) pan with melted butter.

Place 1 sheet of phyllo on the bottom of the prepared pan and brush with melted butter. With scissors, cut another couple sheets (as needed) to place on the sides of the pan, making sure to overlap the edges; brush with melted butter. Repeat 9 more times, for a total of ten layers, being sure to brush the topmost layer.

Stir the custard mixture with a spatula to refresh. Pour mixture into the pan.

In the same way, place 1 sheet of phyllo over the custard mixture and brush with butter. Cut another sheet or two (as needed) for the sides, overlapping the edges and brushing with butter. Repeat 9 more times, being sure to butter the topmost layer. Discard remaining phyllo or repackage and refrigerate for another occasion.

With a sharp knife, trim excess phyllo on the sides of the pan by cutting ¼ inch down from the rim of the pan and working the knife all around; discard. Lightly brush the cut edges with melted butter and place in preheated oven. Bake for 30 minutes. Lower heat to 325 degrees and cook for another 30-35 minutes, or until a golden-honey color. Transfer to a cooling rack. Let set and cool for at least a couple of hours.

After the custard has set and cooled for a couple hours, cut into 3-inch squares using a sharp knife.

Remove cloves and orange peel from syrup; discard. With a large metal spoon, spoon the syrup into all cut edges, including around the perimeter. Sprinkle with ground cinnamon. Serve warm.

Crème Caramel

Many years ago when my mother's sister Bitsa came to visit from Milwaukee, she made this recipe from memory, and my family has been making it ever since. It's not as dense and rich as most. As a matter of fact, this custard is so light and silky it just glides down your throat. The lemon zest adds refreshing flavor and contrasting texture.

If you love custard like I do but have never prepared it before, don't be intimidated. This step-by-step approach—along with a few helpful tips—will embolden you to make it again and again.

Serves 8

Caramel Syrup

1½ cups sugar

6 tablespoons warm water

**2 tablespoons water,
    reserved in a cup**

Custard

**6 cups (1½ quarts) regular or
    2% low-fat milk**

2 teaspoons vanilla extract

6 whole eggs

4 egg yolks

3 teaspoons lemon zest

1 cup sugar

Hot water

For the Caramel Syrup: Set aside 8 (1-cup) ramekins or Charlotte Russe dessert cups.

Set aside an extra-large (17½ x 12 x 3-inch) baking pan.

Pour 1½ cups sugar and 6 tablespoons water in a small, heavy-bottomed pot and stir on medium heat until dissolved. *(Tip: While the sugar dissolves, dip the tips of a pastry brush in the reserved water and wipe the interior sides of the pot. This helps prevent the sides of the pot from forming crystals.)* Increase heat to medium-high and let the mixture come to a boil. Holding the pot handle with an oven mitt, swirl the sugar mixture around until the sugar melts completely and reaches a golden caramel color, about 6-8 minutes. *(Note: Here, the sugar-syrup mixture will first boil, then form crystals, and finally liquefy, getting darker as it cooks. A darkish-brown color means the sugar is developing a bitter burnt taste. If so, start over.)* Remove from heat and pour into ramekins, distributing evenly; set aside.

For the Custard: Position the oven rack to second from the bottom. Preheat oven to 325 degrees.

Pour milk in a medium saucepan and add vanilla; stir. Cook on medium-high heat until just below the boiling point. Remove saucepan from burner; set aside.

In a large bowl, beat whole eggs and egg yolks with an electric mixer for 1 minute. Add lemon zest. Slowly add 1 cup sugar, and beat for 3-4 minutes, or until pale yellow, thick, and frothy. Slowly add hot-milk mixture to egg mixture and blend with a wire whisk until combined well. *(Note: Using a whisk instead of an electric mixer reduces the amount of bubbles that form.)*

Ladle custard mixture into ramekins, distributing evenly. Transfer ramekins to the extra-large pan and place in preheated oven. With a spouted vessel, such as a large measuring cup, pour hot water inside the roasting pan until the water level reaches three-quarters of the way up the ramekin. *(Note: This is called a water bath, or* bain marie. *It sounds so much better in French!)* Bake for 30-35 minutes, or until a toothpick inserted in the center of the custard comes out clean. Transfer to a cooling rack. *(Tip: To avoid burning yourself, use an oven mitt, and from the top of the ramekin, lift it up and out of the pan.)* Transfer to a cooling rack and cool for 10-15 minutes.

Place ramekins in the refrigerator for at least several hours or overnight so the custard can set. To unmold, release the edges of the ramekin with a sharp knife, cover the ramekin with a plate, and flip upside down until the custard and syrup release. Serve cold.

Cranberry Sauce

My paternal *papou* (grandfather) was surely an enterprising fellow. Although his autobiography details a long, illustrious business career, it's page one of this document that interests me most. Here, he describes charming scenes from his boyhood in the country village, and I learn more about my food past.

It starts out like this: "I was born in 1882 in the town of Licouria, in the county of Kalavrita, Greece…. For most of my father's life, he held the office of supervisor in Licouria, but he was also the town butcher and, at the same time, he wholesaled herds of cows, goats, pigs, and sheep and made a nice profit. But his best business venture was organizing bazaar-like fairs. Thousands of people, especially Jewish merchants, came from nearby villages to buy and sell their wares. For these bazaars, my father had to hire many workers while he and the others kept a close eye on the bazaar's sales. My mother, a wonderful cook, would carefully oversee the barbecue pit where at least six delicious lambs were always cooking. During the summer, my father organized about four or five of these fairs in the area."

After my *papou* emigrated to America, his own entrepreneurial spirit blossomed. First, he organized Greek immigrant labor to work on the railways. Then he started the wholesale grocery business in San Francisco. Later, *papou* owned a company that manufactured jams and jellies where apricots, pineapples, peaches and even mincemeat (those same fruit jellies with raisins added) got packed into large containers and sold. Government contracts from World War II spurred his business further.

Ahh, those delectable jams and jelly spreads that can wake up a slice of morning toast! I've been known to drift off in reverie while envisioning myself busy in the kitchen with that quintessential pastime of canning preserves, then dressing their lids with adorable red and white gingham bonnets to give as gifts for family and friends. But so far, the closest I've come is making my Auntie Aspasia's Cranberry Sauce.

The first time I tasted it was around the holidays when she invited my father and me for lunch at her home one year. Needless to say, I loved its interesting flavor and texture, and she kindly sent me the recipe. Its consistency more resembles chutney than the more familiar version. And besides its usual location alongside turkey and stuffing, this makes a tasty sandwich spread, too. Owing to its yummy flavor, Auntie Aspasia wrote, "This recipe did not call for brandy, but I added it to taste, and think it's the ingredient that really makes it. Enjoy!"

Blessed be the ties that bind.

Makes 2 ½ to 3 cups

2 cups, or one (12-ounce) bag fresh cranberries

1 cup orange juice

1 ¾ cups sugar

½ cup white seedless raisins

1 teaspoon grated orange zest

2 tablespoons brandy or whiskey

½ cup slivered almonds

Rinse cranberries in a colander and pat dry with paper towels. Place in a small (2-quart) saucepan and add orange juice. Stir to coat. Cook on medium-high heat until most of their skins have popped, stirring once or twice. Add sugar, raisins, grated orange zest, and brandy or whiskey; stir until combined well. Reduce to medium-low heat and cook, uncovered, for about 20-22 minutes, or until the mixture has thickened, stirring occasionally. Remove pot from fire and add slivered almonds; stir. Adjust to taste. Pour into a ceramic bowl or sterilized jars. Refrigerate until ready to use; serve cold. Stays fresh for at least one month.

Rice Pudding
Rizogalo

This recipe harks back to my childhood. To this day, I still enjoy a warm bowl—it's about as comforting as a mother's tender touch. Maybe that's why rice pudding has such broad appeal—little tykes and savvy adults enjoy it as much as mellow middle-agers and sensible seniors. Plus, it's so versatile. It can be eaten for breakfast, as a snack, or for dessert either warm, cold, or at room temperature. And with a dollop of whipped cream and a sprinkling of ground cinnamon, it can even be served to your most distinguished guests. So next time you've had a hard day, snuggle up with a bowl of rice pudding—before you know it, all will be right with the world.

Serves 6

Rice

1½ cups water

1 tablespoon butter

½ teaspoon salt

¾ cup uncooked long grain white rice

Milk Mixture

1 quart whole or 2% low-fat milk

¾ cup sugar

1 egg yolk

½ teaspoon vanilla extract

Topping

Ground cinnamon

Set aside 6 (1 cup) ramekins.

For the Rice: Pour the water into a small (1-quart) saucepan. Add butter and salt and bring to a boil. Reduce to low heat and add rice; stir. Cover and cook until all the water is absorbed, about 15 minutes; set aside.

For the Milk Mixture: Pour the milk in a medium (3-quart) saucepan and cook on medium-high heat until milk is hot but not boiling. Add sugar and stir until dissolved.

Place egg yolk in a small bowl and beat with a fork. Add to milk mixture, getting every last drop with a spatula.

Add vanilla and cooked rice; stir to combine well. Bring to a boil then reduce heat to low. Cook, uncovered, until mixture becomes thick, about 20 minutes, stirring often. Pour into ramekins and sprinkle with a dash cinnamon. Let cool about 10-15 minutes and serve warm, or refrigerate until ready to eat.

Halva

By now it should be no surprise that I tell you I love to eat.

Apparently, this fact was evident at a young age. As my mother reported to me years later, "I put a basket of strawberries on your high-chair tray, and when I turned around, they were all gone!"

Even in grade school I remember being impatient for the lunch bell to ring so I could discover what my mother had packed that day. Then, I would clutch my tin Barbie lunch pail and dash for the playground.

My favorite sandwich was salami and American cheese (the orange kind) with plenty of mayonnaise, and a crisp leaf of iceberg lettuce. But I enjoyed the others, too—bologna, ham, peanut butter and jelly, and tuna (the egg salad one, though, got tossed—shhh). The best part was the white bread. My mother bought the Kilpatrick's brand that came in a blue and white gingham plastic wrap. Those slices were so soft and fresh I could easily manage an imprint of my thumb and fingers. On the other hand, my best friend Virginia Levy, who lived down the street, got her sandwiches on that brown whole-wheat kind. Besides viewing that as strange, I felt sorry for her.

As for dessert, my mother's growing reputation as a baker meant I could look forward to a Greek sweet or two tucked in with the day's menu. Sometimes I got Twist Cookies with Sesame Seeds *(Koulourakia)*, or Butter Cookies *(Kourambiethes)*. Now and then I also found a slice of homemade halva. My mother usually made halva on a whim. "I feel like making halva today," she would say. Sure enough, thirty minutes later a warm, delicious plate of it would appear.

There are many variations of this sweet confection. Some are made with semolina (a coarse by-product of wheat), some with farina (ground semolina—a common breakfast porridge), and still others from sesame seeds or sesame seed paste (tahini). It can also be made into different forms. Some versions are fancy "cakes" while others are plain. Some are molded into chunks, and others into candy bars. Then there's the endless debate about additives. Nuts? Chocolate? Coconut?

But all in all, the simple one I found in my tin Barbie lunch pail still suits me best.

Serves 8

<u>Syrup</u>

2 cups water

1 cup sugar

1 cinnamon stick

<u>Farina Mixture</u>

½ cup (1 stick) butter

1 cup farina

¼ cup slivered almonds

Ground cinnamon

For the Syrup: Pour water in a small (1½-quart) saucepan and add sugar. Stir over medium high heat until sugar dissolves. Add cinnamon stick and bring to a boil. Reduce heat to low and cook for 5 minutes; set aside.

For the Farina Mixture: Melt butter in a medium (3-quart) saucepan over medium heat. Add farina and almonds and stir continuously with a wooden spoon until combined well. Discard cinnamon stick from syrup; add syrup to farina mixture. Cook until the mixture becomes very thick, about 3 minutes, stirring continuously

Turn mixture onto a 10-inch plate and shape into a smooth mound using the back of a wooden spoon. For a decorative effect, indent the halva with the side of the spoon every few inches, starting from the center. Sprinkle ground cinnamon on top. When ready to serve, cut in wedge-shaped slices as you would a pie. Serve warm, cold, or at room temperature.

Peanut Brittle

Spanish peanuts—with their round kernels and distinct flavor and texture—are especially delicious in this recipe. But if you're having a hard time finding them in the store, the standard variety works well, too.

Whether this is your first time making candy, or you're a seasoned confectionaire, it's important to stay focused when preparing sugar syrup. That's because as the syrup cooks, it goes through different stages of temperature (from low to high) and consistency (from loose, to snowy, to liquid, to hard). As the water boils out of the syrup, the sugar concentration increases as does the temperature, which affects the syrup's formation and color.

There are two ways to assess these stages. One is by using an instant-read thermometer. The other is by doing a cold-water test (described below). Many cooks use both methods. Either way, be prepared (or "test ready") and have whichever means you choose near the stove.

After you're finished, consider packaging this old-fashioned candy in small cellophane bags and tying them with a pretty ribbon for gift-giving around the holidays— but only after stashing some of it for your own sweet pleasure. (Adapted; source unknown.)

Makes 1 batch

1 tablespoon butter (for greasing the pan)

2 cups sugar

1 cup light corn syrup

1 cup water

2 (12.5 ounce) cans salted redskin Spanish peanuts, skins intact

1 tablespoon butter

¼ teaspoon baking soda

1 cup cold water with a couple of ice cubes

Candy thermometer (optional)
1 (7 to 9-inch) glass or porcelain plate

Grease a large (15 x 10 x 1-inch) baking sheet with 1 tablespoon butter; set aside.

Pour sugar, corn syrup, and 1 cup water in a large (5-quart) heavy-bottomed saucepan. Stir over medium-high heat until sugar dissolves and cook for 15-20 minutes, without stirring. *(Note: During this time the mixture will boil, crystallize [become snowy], then*

liquefy producing a light blonde color.) Toward the end of this cooking time, test a few drops in a cup of cold water containing a few ice cubes. When the drops form small balls (called the soft-ball stage), or when a candy thermometer registers 235-245 degrees, add the peanuts. Stir with a wooden spoon to coat. Continue cooking until testing a small amount of the mixture in the same cup of cold water separates into brittle strands (called the hard-crack stage), or when a candy thermometer registers 300-310 degrees. *(Tip: A rich caramel color is a good indicator of doneness. A darkish brown one means the sugar is developing a bitter, burnt taste.)*

Add butter and baking soda; stir. After the butter melts, turn peanut brittle onto the greased baking pan and flatten right away with the backside of a plate. Lift the edges around the perimeter with a spatula to loosen. Cool completely, about 30 minutes. Snap off pieces and store in an airtight container.

Afterword

Five years ago I embarked on a new venture—to write a cookbook to honor my dear mother and share the treasured recipes contained in the yellow, accordion-style case she gave me so long ago. Seasoned with enduring remembrances from my past, this book came to express those things I value most—culture, food, friends, and family. Now we have arrived at the end of our journey.

Perhaps by now you've already started being more organized, engaged, bold and courageous, in charge, and joyful, and as a result, are noticing your dishes tasting lovelier. Maybe you're more at ease with phyllo, or perhaps you've simply enjoyed learning a little about Greek culture. Regardless, I hope *Tradition! Recipes, Tales, and More from My Greek American Life* has in some way whet your appetite and touched your heart.

And so, let this cookbook be a blessing to all. Or, as the booklet of prayer hymns *(akathist)* recites, "May good deeds be multiplied in her name." When we can no longer celebrate the joy of good food with our loved ones, we can celebrate our memories. For our memories bring hope, and hope is eternal.

With Gratitude

Writing this cookbook was indeed a labor of love, and it is with deep gratitude I acknowledge the following people who helped me bring it to fruition:

- Mark Hundley, who kindly taught me how to use iPhoto on my laptop, offered tips on shooting with natural light, and photographed the front and back covers.

- Yvonne Wun, who generously gave of her time and expertise to design this entire book so it could be ready to send to press.

- Jim Baldwin, my developmental editor, for helping me shape my material from a gargantuan pile of stories into a structure that flowed. I heeded all your wise suggestions.

- Bernie Borok, my copyeditor and proofreader. What a relief it was to finally turn this manuscript over to such capable and professional hands.

- Caroline Merchant, my daughter, for inputting all my recipes into the computer and saving me countless hours.

- Brian Cox, our local greengrocer, who so patiently answered endless questions about seasonal fruits and vegetables.

- Dr. Fawad Malik, for your unwavering belief in me, especially in the early and middle stages of this project.

- Adele Fatemi, my cousin, for graciously sharing some of her mother's recipes.

- Alexandra Malakooti, Adele's sister (my other cousin), who helped me with translations from English to Greek. I still hope to one day speak and write fluent Greek.

- Tessie Papageorge, my dear aunt, for helping me to fill the blanks about my family history.

- Heather Herbert, for the same contribution with our family history. You amaze me.

- Lori Farley, Marcia Signori, and Michelle Tandowsky, who generously contributed their yummy recipes to this book.

- Bill, Ann, Steven, Lauren, and Christina Eliopoulos for insisting I include photos of my recipes. It was sure a lot of work, but well worth it.

- Jim, Jayne, and Harrison Walkowiak for all the taste testing and feedback you provided.

- My close girlfriends—you know who you are. You will never know how much your inquiries and encouragement kept me going.

- Sophia Petropoulos, my maternal grandmother; Panagiota Kockos, my paternal grandmother; and Bitsa Topping, Chrys Petropoulos Ciarulo, and Aspasia Downey, my aunts, whose recipes appear in this book. Although you are no longer with us, I think of you every time I use one of them.

- Basil Kockos, my father. Dad, your entrepreneurial spirit taught me to take a risk despite not having all the answers. I think about you every day.

- Maria Petropoulos Kockos, my mother. Mom, there would be no cookbook without you. I miss you dearly, yet you continue to inspire me every day.

- Stephen, Caroline, and Gregory Merchant, our beautiful grown children. What a privilege it is to be your mother—this book is for you. May it bless you, and someday your children and your children's children.

- Steve Merchant, my wonderful husband and number one taste-tester. Your steady presence and support has been invaluable throughout this project just as it has been every day of our marriage. Our dining room table is finally cleared!

Appendix A—Being At Ease with Phyllo

Many people love eating foods made with phyllo, but at the same time are deathly afraid of cooking with this fine pastry dough. Why? "It's too intimidating," they say. Here, I hope to embolden even the most faint of heart.

The truth is, working with phyllo (also spelled filo, or fillo) compares to a task you've already done many times—handling tissue paper when wrapping a gift. How are they alike? Both call for unfolding the stack and using one sheet at a time. Both involve handling each sheet gently so it won't tear or crinkle. And finally, both require gentle tucks and nudges with your fingers and knuckles so it fits properly inside the box or baking pan. Therefore, when you combine your gift-wrapping skills with the following facts and tips about phyllo—plus a dash of experience—you'll naturally be at ease.

Phyllo Facts

Product Information

When cooked, phyllo produces a light and flaky crust that can envelop anything from fruit and cheese to vegetables and meat. The "envelope" can take the shape of a rolled cigar or triangles. It can also be arranged casserole-style, where a bottom and top crust hold a delicious filling, like a double-crust pie.

Whatever mode it takes, phyllo can be purchased fresh at certain ethnic specialty shops, or frozen at your local grocery store. It can also be homemade, but I wouldn't dare try! I buy the frozen kind and am usually very pleased.

Regarding its size, phyllo technically comes in 4 different sizes: #4 (fine and silky), #5, #7, and #10 (a thicker country style). Each size represents that many thousandths of an inch, hence size #4 equals 4 thousandths of an inch, and so forth. But mostly, you'll find sizes #4 or #7 at your local market. Although I've used both, I prefer the delicate yield of #4 (fine and silky). However, for heartier recipes, such as those prepared with meat, size #7 works well, too. *(Note: The size is usually marked on the package.*

Alternatively, it may read "fine" [#4], or "medium" [#7].)

Finally, phyllo is sold by the pound and comes in two lengths, short or long. The short version is 9x14 inches and contains about 40 sheets. The long measures 12x17 inches (or 14x18 inches) and contains 20-24 sheets (for #4) or 14-16 sheets (for #7). I use the longer version for all the recipes in this cookbook.

Shelf Life and Thawing Frozen Phyllo

- The shelf life for an unopened box of fresh or thawed phyllo is about 3-4 weeks (stored in the refrigerator).
- Frozen phyllo will stay good in the freezer for about 6-9 months.
- To thaw frozen phyllo: Place in the refrigerator and let it sit overnight without opening the package. *(Note: Don't thaw it on your kitchen counter; excess moisture might cause the sheets of phyllo to stick together!)*

Uncooked Phyllo Freezes Beautifully

Let's say you've just finished preparing Triangle Cheese Pies *(Tiropites)*. Instead of cooking them right away, you can freeze them instead. How wonderful it is knowing those pans are ready and waiting on the day you entertain!

The Three Essentials

Three essential items need to be on hand when working with phyllo: butter or oil, a pastry brush, and a damp towel.

1. *Melted butter (or oil)* gives phyllo its crisp, flaky texture. I always use either salted or unsalted butter (also called sweet butter), whichever the recipe calls for. Some people prefer to use oil instead. If you're in this camp, I suggest using light-tasting oil, such as vegetable. A stronger tasting one, such as olive oil, may be too robustly flavored for this delicate dough.

2. A *pastry brush* is an indispensable tool for applying the butter/oil to phyllo, and can be purchased at any culinary store. They come in assorted widths. I usually use a

2-inch-wide brush, and find it to be a comfortable size for all the sweeping and gliding motions required. Also, dip just the tips of the brush in the butter or oil. The goal is to wet each sheet liberally, not drench it. As far as cleanup, I recommend using hot water and dishwashing liquid instead of placing your pastry brush in the dishwasher.

3.   After unfolding the phyllo from the package, cover it right away with a *damp towel*. This keeps it moist and protected from oxygen, which causes phyllo to become dry and brittle. Brittle phyllo is a pain—if not an impossibility—to work with. I use a thin cloth, such as a flour sack towel, and mist or sprinkle it with water. (Conversely, a heavy terry cloth towel drenched in water will cause your phyllo to become soggy and difficult to work with, so use discretion in the weight of your cloth and the amount of water you apply.)

Now with some of the fundamentals out of the way, here are a few tips to help the job go smoothly.

Helpful Tips

Tip #1—Make an Assembly Line

Remember the first Be-Attitude of cooking mentioned earlier, Be-Organized? It's especially helpful to be organized when working with phyllo.

As previously stated, when phyllo is exposed to oxygen it becomes dry and brittle. So, once the package is opened and the sheets are unfolded, the last thing you want to be doing is looking for your pastry brush or reaching for the butter inside the refrigerator. It's imperative to be organized and have an assembly line in place. This means placing your melted butter or oil to one side with your pastry brush nearby; having your dampened cloth ready to go; and finally, making sure your prepared pan is close by. After you've set up a system, you're ready to proceed—calmly.

Tip #2—Develop a Rhythm and Stay Focused

When working with phyllo, I find that if I maneuver too quickly, too slowly, or get distracted, all kinds of things can go wrong: The corners of the triangle shapes become sloppy and cockeyed instead of neatly tucked; the sheet gets torn when I yank it from the stack; the butter from the brush spatters everywhere; I forget how many layers of phyllo I've already applied; or, the sheet of phyllo dries up while I'm talking on the phone. So, find a comfortable speed that works for you and stick to it. Then concentrate on the task at hand.

Tip #3—Work with What You've Got ("Good Luck or Bad Luck"?)

Every time my mother made something with phyllo, like *Baklava* or Triangle Cheese Pies *(Tiropites)*, she called me immediately after with a report on the level of ease or difficulty she had with that particular package of phyllo. Mostly, she called to say, "I had good luck with the phyllo." But on occasion, she would call to say, "I had bad luck."

After gaining some experience with phyllo myself, I understood exactly what she meant. When the phyllo is fresh and the sheets separate easily—one by one—the experience is pleasurable (good luck). On the other hand, if they stick together or are dry and brittle (bad luck) you may get so frustrated you'll want to throw the whole thing in the trash. What to do? First, don't give up. Know the problem isn't you, but instead, the card you were dealt (or in this case, the package you purchased). Then, besides praying for the patience of Job, read the following remedies.

- *For sheets that stick together,* the culprit is too much moisture. When this happens, separating them is like trying to open a sealed envelope. And, you know what happens when you try to do that. Despite every effort, it rips all over. So first, attempt to gently slide your hand between the two pieces to see if they separate. If still to no avail, use both sheets. The other option is to cut, paste, and patch (read on).

- *Sheets that break apart easily* signal that the phyllo isn't very fresh. But don't lose heart. Now's the time a pair of scissors never looked lovelier. The common remedy here is to cut, patch, and paste. In other words, cut around the unusable portion, discard that portion, and salvage the part of the sheet that's still good. Then patch that piece with the other phyllo in the pan, and "paste" it in place by brushing melted butter over it. The beautiful thing is, your cutting and pasting will appear seamless. When phyllo gets brushed, it blends into the other layers already in the pan. No one will know the difference! In a word, work with what you've got and persevere.

Tip #4—Wilted, Cooked Phyllo

Phyllo's main attraction is its crisp, featherweight crust. But when cooked phyllo is refrigerated, it can sometimes wilt from condensation. Unfortunately, reheating phyllo in the microwave won't bring it back to life, but don't worry. Phyllo has a magical quality —it pops back into its old, crispy self when it gets reheated in the oven.

To do this, place your phyllo-prepared food in a baking pan and cover it with foil. Place the pan in a preheated oven at 300 degrees and cook until heated through. The last 3-5 minutes of cooking, remove the foil and voilà—crispy phyllo. What a relief it is knowing all is not lost.

Also, when cooked phyllo comes out of the oven, let it cool completely before covering with plastic or foil. Otherwise, the steam will cause the phyllo to wilt.

Now that you're equipped with basic information and helpful tips, you can go forward with confidence and composure. There are many different and delicious foods to prepare and enjoy with this fine pastry dough. You can do it!

Appendix B
A Walk Through the Year:
Your Guide to Seasonal Produce

We've heard it time and again—buying seasonal produce offers the best flavor at the best price. But aside from July's peach and October's pomegranate, I wondered which fruits and vegetables actually constituted those monthly picks, and which were offered year round. Having this information, I reasoned, would not only make meal planning easier, but also reduce some of the angst that accompanies making decisions in the middle of the produce aisle. So, I aimed to find out.

For one year, I searched the bins at local markets and scoured the food section in local newspapers. Though the results (below) are not exclusive, and will vary according to weather and geographical region, I hope it helps with that lingering question "What's for dinner tonight?" *before* you arrive at the store.

Year-Round Produce

Fruits—**Lemons**

Vegetables—**Arugula** (in cool-weather regions), **broccoli, cauliflower, carrots, celery, celery root, chard, dandelions, garlic, green cabbage, green onions** (also called scallions), **kale, leeks, lettuces** (butter, iceberg, green and red leaf, Romaine), **onions,** Anaheim **peppers, potatoes** (also listed below), **spinach,** and **onions** (also listed below).

January

Fruits—The New Year greets with **apples** (all varieties), the **citrus** family (grapefruits, oranges, mandarins, Minneolas [larger than tangerines but smaller than oranges], and the chic Meyer lemon). You'll also find **kiwis** and **winter pears** (Bosc, Comice, and d'Anjou).

Vegetables—In supply are **root vegetables** (parsnips, radishes, rutabagas, and turnips), **Brussels sprouts, cabbage** (all varieties), **collard greens** (a variety of kale), **kohl-rabi** (tastes similar to the broccoli stem, but is milder and sweeter), and **mustard greens** (from the mustard plant). Also good are **fennel** (bulb) and **russet potatoes.** A few varieties of **winter squash** are still available, like spaghetti and acorn.

Other—Herbs: **Cilantro, fennel** (leaves), and **rosemary.** *Nuts:* **Almonds, Brazil, chestnuts,** and **walnuts.**

February

Fruits—Refer to January's listing.

Vegetables—This month's cool and damp weather produces a plethora of **mushrooms** (brown, button, cremini, oyster, and portobello). For adventuresome eaters who enjoy a bitter bite, **winter lettuces** from the chicory family (endive, curly endive [also called frisee], escarole [a variety of endive], and radicchio)—are plentiful. Jumbo **artichokes** make their way into the market. Still in season are **beets, cabbage** (all varieties), **collard greens, fennel, mustard greens, potatoes,** and **radishes.**

Other—Herbs: **Fennel** (leaves).

March

Fruits—**Strawberries** signal the arrival of spring and **avocados** appear in the bins. Otherwise, January and February fruits remain in supply.

Vegetables—The harvest of early spring vegetables includes **baby carrots, green garlic** (mild), edible **pea pods, spring onions** (like fresh green onions, but with a larger bulb), and **stinging nettles** (the sting goes away with cooking). **Asparagus** arrives, so eat up because they're only available for a short two-month season. Also in the bins are **artichokes, English cucumbers, fennel, radishes, rhubarb, and russet Idaho potatoes.** These also remain plentiful: **cabbage** (all varieties), **collard greens, mushrooms** (white button, brown cremini, and portobello), **mustard greens,** and **winter lettuces** from the chicory family (endive, curly endive [also called frisee], escarole [a variety of endive], and radicchio).

Other—Herbs: **Fennel** (leaves) and **parsley.**

April

Fruits—The first crop of apricots arrives. Also good are **avocados, honeydew melons, kiwis,** and **strawberries.** Late-season fruits include **apples, citrus** (grapefruit, mandarins, oranges, and tangerines), and **pears** (Bosc).

Vegetables—The arrival of spring welcomes **artichokes, asparagus, English cucumbers, English peas, fava beans, green beans, green bell peppers, green garlic, spring onions** (like green onions, but with a larger bulb), **sweet onions** (also known as Vidalia, Walla Walla, or Maui), **radishes,** and **zucchini.** Still gracing the bins are **collard greens, mustard greens, potatoes** (fingerling, russet, and Yukon gold), **rhubarb,** and **winter lettuces** (endive, escarole, and radicchio).

May

Fruits—As we head toward summer, **apricots** and **cherries** are the first of the stone fruits that are ripe and delicious. **Berries** (blueberries, blackberries, and strawberries) are abundant. The initial crop of **cantaloupe** arrives from the California desert. **Kiwis** are still good and the price of **red seedless grapes** starts to drop.

Vegetables—May hails in nature's bounty with **artichokes** (jumbo, large, and hearts), **arugula** (peak season, but in some climates is year-round), **beets** (red and gold), **eggplants, English cucumbers, fava beans, green bell peppers, green peas, sweet onions** (also known as Vidalia, Walla Walla, or Maui), and **zucchini.** Also, you'll think you've just walked into **potatoland** with their generous supply in the bins (creamers, fingerling, red, russet, and Yukon gold).

Other—Herbs: **Cilantro.**

June

Fruits—The summer chimes with all the luscious fruits we typically associate with the season: **berries** (blackberries, raspberries, and strawberries), **figs, grapes** (seedless), **melons** (cantaloupe, casaba [like honeydew, but not as sweet], Crenshaw [very sweet and juicy with orange flesh], honeydew, and watermelon), and **stone fruits** (apricots, cherries, nectarines, peaches, and plums).

Vegetables—Most of May's vegetables remain plentiful, but this month you'll also find **beans** (Blue Lake and Romano), **okra, mushrooms** (portobello), and **summer squash** (crookneck, summer, sunburst, and zucchini). **Sweet corn** starts making its way into the market, as do **tomatoes** (cherry, beefsteak, and heirloom).

Other—*Herbs:* **Basil.**

July

Fruits—Summer is in full swing with **avocados, berries** (blackberries, raspberries, and strawberries), **figs, grapes** (red and green), **melons** (all varieties), and **stone fruits** (apricots, cherries, nectarines, peaches, plums, and pluots [a cross between a plum and an apricot]) supplying the bins. The first crop of **Bartlett pears** arrives.

Vegetables—July enchants with **beans** (Blue Lake, Romano, and French), **beets, bell peppers** (green, red, and yellow), **eggplant, English cucumbers, garlic** (peak season), **green peas,** and **sweet corn.** Also delicious are **okra, summer squash** (crookneck, sunburst, summer, yellow, and zucchini), and **tomatoes** (beefsteak, cluster, cherry, grape, and heirloom).

Other—*Herbs:* **Arugula, basil, cilantro, dill, mint,** and **parsley.**

August

Fruits—August continues to offer July's bounty. Now is also peak season for **blackberries, raspberries, and strawberries. Figs,** seedless **grapes** (green and red), **melons** (all varieties), and some **stone fruits** (nectarines, peaches, and plums) are still good. Ripe **Bartlett pears** abound, and watch for shipments of flavorful **papayas** and **pineapples** from Hawaii. The first crop of **apples** arrives.

Vegetables—**Tomatoes** (beefsteak, cherry, cluster, heirloom, and vine-ripe) steal the show for August. **Beans** (Italian and Blue Lake), **green** and **red bell peppers, eggplant, English cucumbers, red potatoes, summer squash** (crookneck, sunburst, and zucchini), and **sweet corn** remain plentiful. Red and gold **beets** are hearty and flavorful. These newcomers nod to the imminent arrival of fall—**Brussels sprouts, cranberry beans** (a shell bean), and **winter squash** (acorn, butternut, kabocha, and spaghetti).

September

Fruits—**Apples, figs, grapes, melons,** and **pears** (all varieties) are plentiful and some **stone fruits** (nectarines, peaches, and plums) linger on the stands. **Pomegranates** (early) and **tangelos** (early) signal the arrival of fall.

Vegetables—September boasts of **artichokes, bell peppers, Brussels sprouts, eggplant, English cucumbers, potatoes** (russet, Yukon, red creamer, and fingerling), **summer squash** (all varieties), **sweet corn,** and **tomatoes.** You'll want to start getting ready for those pies as **pumpkins** start making their way to the market. **Root vegetables** (parsnips, rutabagas, and turnips) mark the cooler weather trend, and **shell beans** (cranberry beans, edamame, and garbanzos) surface in the bins.

October

Fruits—This month you'll find **apples, cantaloupe, citruses** (grapefruit, oranges, tangerines), **cranberries, dates, grapes** (including the global or table variety), **honeydew melons, kiwis, pears, persimmons, pomegranates,** and **quince** (a bright yellow, pear-shaped fruit used mainly for jelly and compote).

Vegetables—October thrives on diversity with these in abundant supply: **artichokes, arugula** (fall harvest), **avocados, beans** (Blue Lake, Italian, and wax), **Brussels sprouts, cabbage** (bok choy, napa, green, red, and Savoy), **eggplant, potatoes** (fingerling, russet, Yukon gold, and creamers), as well as **parsnips, rhubarb, sweet potatoes, turnips, winter squashes** (acorn, banana, butternut, Danish, pumpkin, spaghetti), and **yams.** Also good are **collard greens.**

Other—Early crops of **almonds** and **walnuts** appear this month, and are just as delicious as snacks as they are in salads.

November

Fruits—In addition to October's listing, you'll find **strawberries** (fall harvest in certain locations).

Vegetables—A plethora of choices is available this month: **bell peppers** (green only), **beets, broccolini** (a cross between broccoli and Chinese broccoli), **broccoli rabe** (a green leaf vegetable), **Brussels sprouts, cabbage** (bok choy, green, red, Savoy), **cluster tomatoes, endive, English cucumbers, fennel** (bulbs), **green beans** (Blue Lake and Italian), **mushrooms** (button, chanterelle, and portobello), **onions** (boiling, cipollini [small with a flat appearance], red, sweet [also known as Vidalia, Walla Walla, or Maui], white, and yellow), **parsnips, potatoes** (creamers, fingerlings, red, Russet, Yukon gold), **radishes, rutabagas, shallots, sweet potatoes, turnips, watercress, winter squash** (acorn, butternut, kabocha, and spaghetti), and **yams.**

Other—*Herbs:* **Cilantro, dill, fennel** (leaves), **lemon grass, parsley.** *Nuts:* **Almonds, Brazil, chestnuts, filberts,** and **walnuts.**

December

Fruits—As December introduces itself to winter, you'll find **apples, citruses** (grapefruits, mandarins, oranges, and tangerines), **cranberries, grapes** (including the global or table variety), **kiwis, winter pears** (apple, Bartlett, Bosc, Comice, and d'Anjou), and **pomegranates.**

Vegetables—Refer to November's listing.

Other—Refer to November's listing.

Appendix C
U.S. Cooking Measurements and Conversions

Teaspoons	Tablespoons	Cups	Fluid Ounces	Milliliters
3 tsp	1 Tbsp		½ oz	15 ml
6 tsp	2 Tbsp	⅛ cup	1 oz	30 ml
12 tsp	4 Tbsp	¼ cup	2 oz	50 ml
16 tsp		⅓ cup		75 ml
18 tsp	6 Tbsp		3 oz	
24 tsp	8 Tbsp	½ cup	4 oz	125 ml
30 tsp	10 Tbsp		5 oz	
32 tsp		⅔ cup		150 ml
36 tsp	12 Tbsp	¾ cup	6 oz	175 ml
48 tsp	16 Tbsp	1 cup (one half pint)	8 oz	250 ml
		2 cups (one pint)	16 oz	500 ml
		4 cups (2 pints or 1 quart)	32 oz	1 liter
		16 cups (1 gallon)	128 oz	4 liters

(**Note:** Dash is less than ⅛ teaspoon)

Metric Conversion Tables

Metric to U.S.

1 milliliter (ml)	⅕ tsp
5 ml	1 tsp
15 ml	1 Tbsp
30 ml	1 fluid oz
100 ml	3.4 fluid oz
240 ml	1 cup
1 liter	34 fluid oz
1 liter	4.2 cups
1 liter	2.1 pints
1 liter	1.06 quarts
1 liter	0.26 gallons
1 gram	0.035 oz
100 grams	3.5 oz
500 grams	1.10 pounds
1 kilogram	2.2 pounds
1 kilogram	35 oz

Dry Measures

1 ounce = 28.35 grams	1 pound = 16 ounces = 454 grams
1 gram = 0.035 ounce	1 kilo = 2.2 pounds = 1,000 grams

Conversion Formulas

To Convert	Multiply	By
Ounces to grams	the ounces	28.35
Grams to ounces	the grams	0.035
Liters to U.S. quarts	the liters	0.95
U.S. quarts to liters	the quarts	1.057
Inches to centimeters	the inches	2.54
Centimeters to inches	the centimeters	0.39

Oven Temperature Conversions

Fahrenheit	Celsius	Gas Mark
250 degrees F	120 degrees C	1
300	150	2
325	165	3
350	180	4
375	190	5
400	200	6
425	220	7
450	230	8
475	240	9
500	250	10

Notes and Bibliography

Notes

Akathist to Jesus Christ: For a Loved One Who has Fallen Asleep (Arizona, 2003), 16.

Bittman, Mark, "The Four Principles of Kitchen Confidence," *Better Homes and Gardens* (March 2011), 165.

Burrell, Jackie, "Google Cooks Up New Recipe Search," *San Jose Mercury News* (March 2, 1011), 1.

Wooden, John, radio interview; source unknown.

Erdos, Joseph, "What's the Difference Between Sweet Potatoes and Yams?" *Huffington Post* (November 16, 2011). www.huffingtonpost.com/2011/11/16difference-between-sweet-potatoes-and-yams_n_1097840.html.

"Essence," *Merriam-Webster,* www.merriam-webster.com/dictionary/essence.

"Cozy," *The Free Dictionary,* www.thefreedictionary.com/cozy.

Bibliography

Akathist to Jesus Christ: For a Loved One Who has Fallen Asleep. Arizona: St. Paisius Serbian Orthodox Monastery, 2003.

Bittman, Mark, "The Four Principles of Kitchen Confidence," *Better Homes and Gardens* (March 2011): 165.

"Bucatini," *Wikipedia,* last modified October 30, 2011, accessed January 21, 2012, http://en:wikipedia.org/wiki/Bucatini.

Burrell, Jackie, "Google Cooks Up New Recipe Search," *San Jose Mercury News* SV Life Food and Wine Section (March 2, 2011): 1.

"Cabbage," *Wikipedia*, last modified May 2012, accessed May 2012, http://en. wikipedia.org/wiki/Cabbage.

"Cannellini Beans," *Cannellini*, accessed January 13, 2012, www.cannellini.com.

"Cannellini Beans," *Cookthink*, accessed January 13, 2012, www.cookthink.com/ reference/988Cannellini_beans_vs_ Great_Northern_beans_vs_Navy_beans.

"Cozy," *The Free Dictionary*, accessed July 26, 2015, www.thefreedictionary.com/cozy.

"Creamer Potato," *Recipe Tips*, accessed January 13, 2012, www.recipetips.com/ glossary-term/t-35863/creamer-potato.asp.

"Creamer Potato," *Wikipedia*, last modified December 10, 2008, accessed January 13, 2012, http://en.wikipedia.org/wiki/Creamer_potato.

"Crème Caramel," *Wikipedia*, last modified July 5, 2015, accessed January 21, 2012, http://en.wikipedia.org/wiki/Crème_caramel.

"The Difference Between Brown Rice and White Rice," *FitDay*, Copyright 2000-2011, accessed April 20, 2013, http://fitday.com/fitness-articles/nutrition/healthy-eating/ the-difference-between-brown-rice-and-white-rice.html#b.

"Essence," *Merriam-Webster*, accessed July 26, 2015, www.merriam-webster.com/ dictionary/essence.

"Greek Olives," Gaifyllia, Nancy, *About.com*, accessed January 19, 2014, http://greek food.about.com/od/greekfoodphotogalleries/ig/Greek-Olive-Photos/.

Hionidou, Violetta. *Famine and Death in Occupied Greece: 1941-1944.* New York: Cambridge University Press, 2006.

Hoffman, Susanna, in Collaboration with Victoria Wise. *The Olive and The Caper: Adventures in Greek Cooking.* New York: Workman Publishing, 2004.

"How to Use a Candy Thermometer – Candy Temperature Chart," *What's Cooking America,* accessed June 10, 2015, http://whatscookingamerica.net/Candy/candy temp.htm.

Ingram, Christine. *The Cook's Encyclopedia of Vegetables.* Leicester, England: Lorenz Books, 1996.

Jensen, Bernard. *Foods That Heal.* New York: Avery, 1988.

Kochilas, Diane. *The Food and Wine of Greece: More Than 300 Classic and Modern Dishes from the Mainland and Islands of Greece.* New York: St. Martin's Press, 1990.

Lindberg, Fedon Alexander, MD. *Eating the Greek Way: More Than 100 Fresh and Delicious Recipes from Some of the Healthiest People in the World.* New York: Clarkson Potter, 2006.

Lumley, Joanna. *Greek Odyssey: The Land of the Ancient Greeks,* Episode #101H. PBS.

"The Many Health Benefits of Dandelion," Peter Gail, *The Leaf Lady,* copyright 1988-2011, accessed March 16, 2014, www.leaflady.org/health_benefits_of_ dandelions.htm.

May, Rollo. *The Courage to Create.* New York: W.W. Norton and Company, Inc., 1975.

Mazower, Mark. *Inside Hitler's Greece: The Experience of Occupation, 1941-44.* New Haven, CT: Yale University Press, 1993.

"Mediterranean Diet," *Wikipedia,* last modified January 26, 2012, accessed January 27, 2012, http//en.wikipedia.org/wiki/Mediterranean_diet.

Milona, Marianthi. ed., *Culinaria Greece: Greek Specialties.* Brandenburg, Germany: h.f. ullmann, 2008.

Ostmann, Barbara Gibbs and Baker, Jane L. *The Recipe Writer's Handbook: Revised and Expanded.* New Jersey: John Wiley & Sons, Inc., 2001.

"Pasta Glossary," Great Chicago Italian Recipes, Copyright 2010, accessed January 21, 2012, www.great-chicago-italian-recipes.com/pasta_glossary.html.

"Pasta Glossary," *The Nibble*, Lifestyle Direct, Inc. 2005-2012, accessed January 21, 2012, www.thenibble.com/reviews/main/pastas/glossary2.asp.

Poffley, Frewin. *Greek Island Hopping 2010.* United Kingdom: Thomas Cook Publishing, 2010.

The Recipe Club of Saint Paul's Greek Orthodox Cathedral. *The Complete Book of Greek Cooking.* New York: Harper Perennial, 1990.

"Roasting Walnuts," *My Home Cooking*, copyright 2008, accessed January 14, 2012, www.myhomecooking.net/chocolate-chip-cookies/roasting-walnuts.htm.

Schubert, Sister. *Cast Your Bread Upon the Waters: Recipes for Success, Cooking, and Living.* Florida: the idea boutique, 2009.

Watson, Betty. *Miracle in Hellas: The Greeks Fight On.* New York: The MacMillan Company, 1943.

"What Is the Difference Between a Sweet Potato and a Yam?" *North Carolina Sweet Potatoes*, accessed January 11, 2016, www.ncssweetpotatoes.com/sweet-potatoes-101/difference-between-yam-and-sweet-potato.

"What's the Difference Between Sweet Potatoes and Yams?" Erdos, Joseph, *The Huffington Post*, Huffpost Taste, posted November 16, 2011 and last modified September 12, 2012, accessed November 12, 2012, www.huffingtonpost.com/2011/11/16difference-between-sweet-potatoes-and-yams_n_1097840.html.

Zinovieff, Sofka, *Eurydice Street: A Place in Athens.* London: Granata Books, 2004.

Index

Note: Greek words are indicated by *italics*.

Maria Petropoulos Kockos
1927-2013